Type 2 Diabetes Cookbook for Beg

Start to Understand and Manage Your Glucose Through a Journey to Discover Low Sugar Mouthwatering Recipes and Improve Your Vitality | Centaurs Method

TABLE OF CONTENTS

1 INTRODUCTION

1.1 What Is Diabetes

Having a high blood glucose level, often known as high blood sugar, could develop diabetes. Your body's primary energy source is blood glucose, which is derived from the food you eat. The pancreas makes the hormone insulin, which makes it easier for your cells to absorb glucose from food and use it as fuel. Sometimes your body doesn't generate any insulin, produces too little insulin, or uses insulin improperly. Following that, glucose does not enter your cells and instead stays in your bloodstream. Over time, having too high blood glucose levels might lead to health issues. Despite the fact that there is no cure for diabetes, you can manage it and stay healthy.

Sometimes, the term "borderline diabetes" or "a touch of sugar" is used to describe diabetes. These statements suggest that a person does not genuinely have diabetes or that they have a less serious ailment. However, diabetes always has serious repercussions.

1.2 What is insulin resistance?

Insulin resistance is a disorder where cells in your muscles, fat, and liver do not respond well to insulin and are unable to use the blood's glucose for energy. In order to make up for the loss, your pancreas makes extra insulin. Over time, your blood glucose levels rise.

Type 2 diabetes, hypertension, excessive cholesterol, and obesity are just a few of the issues that are part of the insulin resistance syndrome. One in three Americans may be impacted. Metabolic syndrome is another name for it.

1.3 What is immunosuppress?

Immunocompromised is defined as, by the National Cancer Institute of the National Institutes of Health, "immune system being compromised Immunocompromised patients are less able to fight off infections and other illnesses. This could be brought on by specific illnesses or situations like AIDS, cancer, diabetes, malnutrition, or specific genetic problems. Radiation therapy, stem cell or organ transplants, radiation therapy for cancer, and other medications or therapies may also contribute to it. Likewise known as immunosuppressed."

The immune system can become weakened by chronically high blood glucose and out-of-range levels, making patients more susceptible to sickness and its complications. Having diabetes does not cause immune system weakness. Immunocompromised individuals may not have type 1 diabetes but may be more susceptible to disease consequences if their diabetes is poorly managed. People with persistently high blood sugar levels (hyperglycemia) and concomitant chronic conditions like heart disease or asthma are most at risk. There isn't enough information to say whether persons with type 1 or type 2 diabetes have different results.

1.4 What are the types of diabetes and their characteristics & differences?

The three primary subtypes of the disease are diabetes type 1, type 2, and gestational diabetes (diabetes while pregnant).

Diabetes type 1

It is believed that type 1 diabetes is brought on by autoimmune reactions (the body attacks itself by mistake). As a result, your body stops producing insulin. Type 1 diabetes affects five to ten percent of people with diabetes. Type 1 diabetes symptoms frequently appear suddenly. Young adults, adolescents, and children are frequently given the diagnosis. You need to take insulin every day to stay alive if you have type 1 diabetes. Currently, type 1 diabetes is uncontrollable.

The origin of type 1 diabetes

The body's immune system defends against external intruders, including dangerous viruses and bacteria. It is thought that type 1 diabetes is brought on by an immune reaction. The immune system of a person with type 1 diabetes mistakenly views healthy cells from their own body as foreign invaders.
The pancreatic beta cells that make insulin are attacked by and destroyed by the immune system. If these beta cells are eliminated, the body is no longer able to create insulin.
Why the immune system occasionally targets the body's own cells is unknown. Other environmental and genetic factors, as well as virus exposure, may have an impact.
Ongoing research is being done on autoimmune diseases. Diet and lifestyle decisions do not cause type 1 diabetes.

Type 2 Diabetes

It can be difficult for your body to use insulin correctly and regulate blood sugar levels if you have type 2 diabetes. 90% to 95% of people with type 2 diabetes experience symptoms. Most persons who have it are diagnosed with it after years of development (but more and more in children, teens, and young adults). If you're at risk, it's critical to get your blood sugar checked because you might not show any symptoms. A healthy lifestyle change can either delay or prevent type 2 diabetes.

- Loss of weight.
- consuming wholesome food.
- starting to move.
- Maternal Diabetes

Even in expectant mothers who have never had gestational diabetes, it can still happen. Having gestational diabetes may make your unborn child more susceptible to health issues. Normally, gestational diabetes goes away once your baby is delivered. It does, however, raise your chance of developing type 2 diabetes in the future. The likelihood that your child may develop type 2 diabetes while still a young child or adolescent due to obesity is higher.

Type 2 diabetes reasons

Insulin resistance is a problem that is related to type 2 diabetes. The body cannot appropriately utilize insulin even while it is still being produced. Researchers are still trying to figure out why some people acquire insulin resistance, and others do not, despite the fact that a variety of lifestyle factors, like being overweight and inactive, may be related. There may be other genetic and environmental factors that are significant. Your pancreas will try to compensate for your type 2 diabetes by producing more insulin. Because your body can't effectively use insulin, glucose builds up in your bloodstream.

Prediabetes

In the United States, 96,000,000 adults, or more than one in three, have prediabetes. More than 80% of them are not even aware of it. Blood sugar levels that are elevated but not high enough to be categorized as type 2 diabetes are the hallmark of prediabetes. If you have prediabetes, you run a higher risk of developing type 2 diabetes, heart disease, and stroke. However, there is good news. You can actively reverse prediabetes with the aid of a CDC-recognized lifestyle change program.

What are the differences between type 1 and type 2 diabetes?

While it can affect adults, type 1 diabetes frequently first manifests in children and teenagers. In those with type 1 diabetes, the immune system destroys the beta cells in the pancreas, which stops them from producing insulin.

Typically inherited, type 1 diabetes cannot be prevented. 5- 10% of patients with diabetes have type 1 diabetes.

Type 2 diabetes can still affect young people, but as they become older, it is more likely to do so. In this type, insulin is produced by the pancreas but is improperly used by the body. Its development appears to be influenced by lifestyle variables. Type 2 diabetes affects the majority of patients with the disease. Both types of diabetes can cause consequences like blood vessel and organ damage, renal disease, eyesight loss, neurological disorders, and cardiovascular and kidney illnesses.

Nearly 25% of Americans who may have diabetes, which affects more than 34 million people, may not even be aware of it.

1.5 What causes and symptoms of Type 2 Diabetes

What causes Type 2 diabetes?

When the pancreas produces less insulin than the body requires and the body cells stop responding to insulin, type 2 diabetes occurs. They do not consume sugar as they ought to. Your blood sugar increases over time. Insulin resistance is a condition when insulin fails to cause cells to react. It is frequently caused by:

- Lifestyle factors, such as inactivity and obesity.
- Faulty genes prohibit cells from functioning normally due to genetics.

What signs and symptoms are present in type 2 diabetes?

Diabetes type 2 symptoms typically appear gradually over time. They may consist of:

- distorted vision
- Fatigue.
- Being really thirsty or hungry.
- Increased urination frequency (usually at night).
- Cut or sore healing takes time.
- Numbness or tingling in your feet or hands.
- Unaccounted-for weight loss

1.6 What are the types of Type 2 Diabetes disease?

According to functional medicine, there may be four different forms of diabetes that go by the name "Type 2." In a recent webinar, functional medicine practitioner Brian Mowll discussed the four categories.

The Institute for Functional Medicine, a global medical organization about which you can read more at this website, has certified Dr. Mowll even though his Ph.D. is in chiropractic, not medicine, and he is also a qualified diabetes educator. He said the following:

About 50% to 60% of all identified cases are Type O, which is the standard Type 2. Type Os have rounder bellies and are hefty. They are very resistant to insulin. Additionally, they have high insulin levels and a lot of insulin production up until the end of the disease.

Type I is frequently thought of as a "thin" Type 2. Low insulin levels and being underweight are possible in subtype I patients. Although they are typically referred to as Type 2, they have high blood glucose and could be diagnosed with LADA (latent autoimmune diabetes of adults).

Hormonal subtype H is referred to. People with subtype H frequently have underactive adrenal glands and low thyroid levels. They frequently have a normal or slightly overweight weight, are prone to inflammation, and may or may not have insulin resistance.

S stands for the stress-induced subtype. It might result from a single dramatic, high-stress traumatic experience or long-term chronic stress. High quantities of the stress chemicals cortisol and adrenaline are present in the bodies of those with subtype S. Blood sugar levels are increased by these hormones.

It is possible to have more than one of these categories, according to Dr. Mowll. The majority of people most likely do.

1.7 What are the symptoms of type 2?

The sensation of feeling sluggish and low on energy

Your energy levels may fall after you get type 2 diabetes, as was previously discussed. People with type 2 diabetes who have just received a diagnosis say they feel exhausted, according to the American Diabetes Foundation. Insufficient amounts of sugar are getting to the cells from the blood, which is the cause of this weariness.

Chronically high blood sugar levels are a symptom of type 2 diabetes, but the sugar has problems getting into your cells. The cells function less efficiently because they lack sufficient energy. As a result, someone with type 2 diabetes could always feel tired.

An excessive thirst

People with type 2 diabetes frequently experience thirst. Polydipsia, the medical term for this abnormal thirst, is caused by an excess of sugar in the blood. In order to get rid of the extra sugar, your kidneys, an important component of the urinary system, must make more effort. Frequent urination is a further early indicator of type 2 diabetes brought on by this.

Your body loses a lot of water when you have frequent urination. You experience a strong urge to hydrate continuously in order to replace the lost fluids. While waiting for the blood sugar levels to equal out, the cycle of urination and thirst can become normal.

Vision Is Hazy

Your eyesight may be blurry as a symptom of type 2 diabetes. One of the more typical signs of type 2 diabetes is eye impairment. The lens of the eye, a vital component of the human eye that focuses light and images into the rest of the eye, will eventually become filled with water from the body as a result of persistently high blood sugar levels. Injuries to the eye's tiny blood vessels are also possible.

If you experience this symptom, you should consult a physician right away. If this problem is not handled right away, permanent eye damage may result.

Continuous Hunger

People with type 2 diabetes may experience constant hunger as well as chronic thirst. Cells lose energy when they are unable to access the bloodstream's supply of sugar. Someone with type 2 diabetes may experience constant hunger until, to recoup some energy, blood sugar levels must return to normal.

It makes no difference how much or lately you ate. You will frequently feel hungry if you have type 2 diabetes because the food you have already eaten is not providing you with enough energy.

1.8   Why is it necessary to treat these problems with the diet

If you have diabetes or prediabetes, your doctor will likely advise you to work with a nutritionist to help you develop a healthy eating plan. The program helps you regulate your weight, blood pressure, blood fat levels, and blood sugar (glucose) levels—all of which are risk factors for heart disease. You don't want your blood sugar to increase because of more calories and fat. Uncontrolled blood glucose levels can result in serious problems, including high blood sugar (hyperglycemia), which, if it persists, may have long-term effects like damage to the heart, kidneys, and nerves.

You can keep your blood glucose levels within a safe range by choosing nutritious meals and monitoring your eating habits. Along with numerous other health advantages, most people with type 2 diabetes find that maintaining their blood glucose levels is easier when they lose weight. If you need to lose weight, a diabetes diet offers a well-thought-out, healthy plan to help you reach your objective.

1.9   What are the characteristics of the Type 2 Diabetes diet?

If you have diabetes, it's very important to maintain a regular eating schedule. Your meal plan will include how much you should consume of each food group, such as carbohydrates, to ensure you meet your daily needs. You'll learn how to keep track of your carb intake and keep a food diary.

Consuming food at the right times of the day is also essential. Planning for regular, balanced meals might help keep blood sugar levels stable. Maintaining a consistent carbohydrate intake across meals can have positive effects.

Your diet plan should also include guidance on how to implement the guidelines you've set for yourself in social situations, such as dining out.

Maintaining healthy blood sugar levels through diet does need effort. The upside, however, is that you can control your diabetes and continue leading a normal, healthy life.

2   FOOD LIST: PERMITTED FOOD, FOOD TO AVOID

Vegetables

A healthy diet is based on vegetables. They are great providers of fiber, vitamins, and minerals.

Many veggies contain fiber and complex carbs that can aid in satiety. This, in turn, may deter binge eating, which can lead to blood sugar issues and weight gain. Several vegetables to include on your grocery list are

- peppers
- tomatoes
- broccoli
- corn
- green peas
- carrots
- greens
- potatoes

Legumes and beans

Beans, lentils, and other pulses are great options for nutritional fiber and protein.

The high fiber component of meals from the pulse family helps the digestive system absorb less carbohydrates than diets with low fiber and high carbohydrate content.

As a result, these foods are excellent sources of carbs for people with diabetes. Additionally, They can be used in place of cheese or meat. The following bean varieties are available in both dried and tinned form:

White beans, kidney beans, pinto beans, black beans, garbanzo beans, lentils, and other beans

Furthermore, boiling beans slowly or under pressure may make them more digestible.

Fruit

Fruit can contain a lot of sugar; however, whole fruit's sugar does not count toward free sugars. Consequently, those who have diabetes shouldn't avoid fruit. The following fruits are a fantastic addition to anyone with type 2 diabetes' diet because of their low glycemic index (GI) and glycemic load:

- grapefruit
- blackberries
- peaches
- pears
- plums
- strawberries
- avocado
- cherries
- apples

Whole grains

Given that they frequently have a lower GI, whole grains can be a useful tool for managing blood glucose levels in diabetics.

People should choose some of the following grains while ingesting grains rather than bleached and processed carbs like white bread and pasta:
• Amaranth • Quinoa • Millet • Wild rice • Cornmeal • Barley • 100% whole-grain or whole-wheat flour
• Oatmeal • Whole-grain bread with at least 3 grams of fiber per slice
Additionally, whole grains may have more flavor and make a person feel fuller longer than processed carbohydrates.

Dairy

Dairy products include calcium and protein, two crucial nutrients. According to several studies, dairy consumption can increase insulin secretion in some type 2 diabetics. Among the best foods to include in one's diet are:

- Greek or plain yogurt,
- low-fat or skimmed milk,
- and parmesan, ricotta, or cottage cheese

Proteins from meat are crucial for diabetics.

Similar to diets high in fiber and fat, proteins take a while to digest and barely affect blood sugar levels. Several excellent sources of protein are as follows:
salmon, sardines, tuna, and other oily seafood, as well as skinless, boneless chicken breast or strips
white fillets of fish
turkey breast eggs without skin
In terms of plant-based proteins, beans, and bean products like:

- baked or refried beans
- peas
- edamame
- tempeh
- hummus
- falafel
- lentils
- black beans
- kidney beans
- pinto beans
- tofu

Condiments, spices, and dressings

For people attempting to control their blood sugar, a variety of seasonings and dressings might be very beneficial.
People with diabetes have the following tasty options to choose from:

- vinegar
- mustard, any type of extract, and any spice or herb
- spiciness salsa
- Using equal parts Making a vinaigrette by combining olive oil and balsamic vinegar (or another vinegar) in equal parts, season to taste with salt, pepper, mustard, and herbs.

Don't forget to take a dressing's carbohydrates into consideration.

Before purchasing any of these items, carefully read the nutrition facts label because certain salad dressings, ketchup, and barbecue sauces may also include a lot of fat, sugar, or both.

Dessert dishes

Desserts are acceptable for those with type 2 diabetes, but they should be consumed sparingly and in moderation.

The following low-calorie or low-carbohydrate choices affect blood sugar levels less than typical sweets:

- Fruit-based sweets, including homemade fruit salad or summer fruit medleys without added sugar, can be a filling and healthy way to end a meal.
- Popsicles without any added sugar are another option.
- Dessert alternatives include sugar-free gelatin pudding or ice cream as well as 100% fruit popsicles.

However, it is essential to take fruit's sugar into consideration when calculating carbohydrates.

Solutions for diabetes without sugar

Diabetes patients must restrict their sugar intake. Foods without sugar may nevertheless have an impact on someone's blood sugar levels.

"Sugar-free" refers to the absence of added sugar in a food product; nevertheless, the product itself may still include carbs, which might affect blood glucose levels.

In this regard, sugar alcohols are one example. These low-calorie sweeteners are frequently used by manufacturers in sugar-free gum, chocolates, ice cream, and fruit spreads. Examples comprise:

- Erythritol
- Sorbitol
- Xylitol
- Maltitol

These different carbohydrate kinds may cause blood sugar levels to rise.

Alternatives to sugar could be chosen. Blood sugar levels are frequently unaffected by a single intake of a sugar substitute.

Common substitutes for sugar include:

- Aspartame
- advantame
- stevia
- Neotame
- saccharin
- sucralose

Snacks

Those who experience cravings in between meals can try:

- • homemade popcorn; unsweetened nuts; unprepared or sweetened varieties.
- Moderate portions of fresh fruit with a protein or fat, like an apple and nut butter;
- Carrot or celery sticks with hummus;

Drinking

- Everyone, even those with diabetes, benefits from drinking water.
- Although there are other reasons, high-carbohydrate beverages like milk and juice may have an impact on someone's blood sugar. It is vital to take these into account, just like with eating.

A person with diabetes might want to consider the following alternatives:

- Unsweetened coffee, skim or low-fat milk;
- Iced tea or hot tea without sugar;
- Sparkling water;
- Plant-based milk without sugar

Limit or stay away from certain meals

People with type 2 diabetes should limit or avoid the same foods that are bad for individuals without the disease. They should also avoid foods and beverages that have a negative impact on blood sugar levels (candies, ice cream, and cakes include simple carbohydrates, trans fats, and sugar).

Individuals should limit their intake of packaged and fast foods such as sweets, candies, chips, and baked goods (white pasta, white rice, white bread, sweet cereals, red meat, and processed meat).

It's also a good idea to avoid low-fat items that use sugar instead of fat. Yogurt sans fat is a good example. Try substituting some of your favorite foods with healthier ones if you have prediabetes or type 2 diabetes. This can entail selecting whole-wheat pasta, bread, or rice and swapping out white potatoes for sweet potatoes or yams. The greatest solution is frequently to create your own meals because it is simpler to get rid of the excess sugars that are included in many prepared foods.

3 FAQ

What are sources of carbohydrates okay for type 2 diabetes?

Beans. All types of beans and legumes are fantastic options because they contain substantial amounts of fiber and protein, two nutrients essential for regulating blood sugar levels.

Quinoa, oats, Greek yogurt, fruits high in fiber,

For type 2 diabetics, is a ketogenic diet safe?

According to a research study, the keto diet is great for managing Type 2 diabetes since it lowers blood sugar and promotes weight loss.

What other moniker would you use for type 2 diabetes?

Although type 2 diabetes is commonly diagnosed in adults, it can also affect children and teenagers. Diabetes that develops in adults is another name for it. Because the body uses the hormone insulin incorrectly, type 2 diabetes is characterized by high blood sugar (glucose) levels.

Diabetes of type 1 and type 2 varieties differ from one another.

Juvenile diabetes, often known as type 1 diabetes, is caused by an ineffective pancreas in children that generates little to no insulin. Type 2 diabetes, on the other hand, which is typically diagnosed later, was formerly known as adult-onset diabetes. In persons with type 2 diabetes, the body has a harder time absorbing and utilizing the insulin that the pancreas produces.

4 SHOPPING LIST FOR A WEEK OF DIET

- yellow or green squash or zucchini
- fresh mozzarella cheese
- olive oil
- fresh or frozen vegetables or both
- bell pepper
- wild-caught salmon fillet
- coffee
- black pepper
- salt
- 1–2% milk
- a salad bag
- unsweetened, olive oil-base dressing
- walnuts, almonds, or other raw nuts
- Parmesan cheese
- corn
- wild rice mix
- tomatoes
- whole strawberries
- onion
- honey
- reduced-sodium soy sauce
- cucumber
- unsweetened almond or flax milk
- apples
- olive oil spray
- sweet potatoes
- low sugar, low sodium barbecue sauce
- boneless, skinless chicken breasts
- fresh basil
- romaine lettuce

5   BREAKFAST RECIPES

5.1   Milk with Overnight Oats

Preparation: 10 minutes

Cooking time: 00 minutes

Servings: 4

Ingredients

- agave nectar (Optional)- 2 tbsp.(30 g)
- lemon zest -1 tsp.(4 g)
- low-fat milk-2 cups (400 ml)
- vanilla extract -½ tsp. (2g)
- fresh apricots, chopped -2
- pine nuts -⅓ cup (46 g)
- rolled oats -2 cups (160 g)

Preparation

1. In a big container, add milk, oats, lemon zest, and vanilla extract. For eight to twelve hours, or when the oats have absorbed the milk, cover and refrigerate the dish.
2. Oatmeal should be combined with apricots, pine nuts, and agave nectar.

Nutrition Information

Calories 293, Fat 11.7g, Total Carbohydrate 37.4g, Total Sugars 8.8g,Protein 11.3g, Potassium 446mg, Sodium 57 mg

Storage For up to five days, place the jar's lid on and store in the fridge.

Reheat: just defrost at room temperature for a few hours

5.2   Apple Muffins

Preparation: 15 minutes

Cooking time: 25 minutes

Servings: 12

Ingredients

- 2/3 cup skim milk (160 ml)
- 1 1/2 cups all-purpose flour (200 g)
- 1/2 teaspoon sea salt (2 g)
- 1/4 teaspoon nutmeg (1 g)
- Lightly beaten egg -1
- 1 cup of minced apple (85 g)
- 2 1/2 teaspoons of baking powder (10 g)
- 1 teaspoon stevia (15 g)
- Melted low-calorie margarine, 1/4 cup (60 g)
- Cooking oil-based spray
- 1 teaspoon of ground cinnamon (4 g)

Preparation

1. Set oven to 400 degrees Fahrenheit. Cooking spray should be used to prepare 12 muffin tins.
2. Combine the flour, baking soda, stevia, cinnamon, sea salt, and nutmeg in a separate bowl. Mix the skim milk, egg, and margarine in a separate bowl. Combine the wet and dry ingredients, only moistening the dry ingredients slightly. Mix the apple mince gently into the batter. With the prepared batter, fill the muffin cups.
3. About 25 minutes into the preheated baking time, the tops should be gently browned.

Nutrition Information

Calories 119 ,Fat 4.4g ,Total Carbohydrate 17.4g,Total Sugars 2.7g , Protein 2.8g, Potassium 173 mg, Sodium 136 mg

Storage: To keep muffins fresh for up to 4 days, line a zip-top bag or airtight container with paper towels and arrange the muffins in a single layer.

Reheat: just defrost at room temperature for a few hours

5.3 Lemon Avocado Toast

Preparation: 10 minutes
Cooking time: 03 minutes
Servings: 2

Ingredients

- 1 pinch fine sea salt
- Cilantro, or more to taste -2 tbsp. (30 g)
- Avocado -½
- chia seeds -¼ tsp.(1g)
- Meyer lemon zest - ¼ tsp. (1 g)
- whole grain bread -2 slices
- Meyer lemon juice, or to taste -1 tsp. (4g)
- 1 pinch cayenne pepper

Preparation

1. Toasted bread slices should be done in 3 to 5 minutes, depending on preference.
2. In a bowl, combine the mashed avocado, cilantro, Meyer lemon zest, cayenne pepper, and sea salt. The avocado mixture is spread over the toast before the chia seeds are added.

Nutrition Information

Calories 170, Fat 10.9g, Total Carbohydrate 17.4g, Total Sugars 2.3g, Protein 4g, Potassium 252mg, Sodium 57 mg

Storage: The avocado mash should be kept separate and in a sealed container.

Reheat: just defrost at room temperature for a few hours

5.4 Spinach Egg White Muffins

Preparation: 10 minutes
Cooking time: 20 minutes
Servings: 10

Ingredients

- Cooking spray
- Hot sauce -1 tsp. (4 g)
- spinach, thawed and drained -1 (10 ounces) package (280 g)
- Ground black pepper -½ tsp. (2g)
- Shredded reduced-fat sharp Cheddar cheese, or more to taste -6 ounces (170 g)
- Salt -1 tsp. (4g)
- Liquid egg whites -2 (4 ounces) cartons (230 g)

Preparation

1. Adjust the oven's temperature at 350 F. (175 degrees C).A muffin pan needs to be sprayed with cooking spray.
2. In a bowl, mash together the egg whites with the Cheddar cheese, spinach, spicy sauce, salt, and pepper. Fill each cup in the muffin tin about 3/4 full as you pour the mixture in.
3. Bake in a preheated oven for 20 to 25 minutes or until a knife inserted in the center of a muffin comes out clean. Serve the food hot or cold.

Nutrition Information

Calories 68,Fat 3.8g, Total Carbohydrate 1.7g, Total Sugars 0.1g, Protein 7.5g , Potassium 160mg, Sodium 444 mg

Storage: To keep muffins fresh for up to 4 days, line a zip-top bag or airtight container with paper towels and arrange the muffins in a single layer.

Reheat: Just defrost at room temperature for a few hours

5.5 Overnight Light Peanut Butter Oats

Preparation: 05 minutes
Cooking time: 00 minutes
Servings: 1

Ingredients

- peanut butter -2 tbsp. (30 g)
- chia seeds -1 ½ tsp. (6g)
- almond milk -½ cup (120 ml)
- rolled oats -¼ cup (20 g)

- fresh raspberries -¼ cup (30 g)
- stevia -1 tsp. (4g)

Preparation

1. Combine stevia, chia seeds, rolled oats, powdered peanut butter, raspberries, and almond milk in a bowl. 8 to overnight, Up till the oats are mushy, cover, and refrigerate.

Nutrition Information

Calories 461 , Fat 33.5g, Total Carbohydrate 32.8g, Total Sugars 10.2g, Protein 12.3g, Potassium 481mg, Sodium 20 mg

Storage: In the refrigerator for up to five days, secure the jar's lid.

Reheat: just defrost at room temperature for a few hours

5.6 Milk with Peaches quinoa

Preparation: 10 minutes

Cooking time: 00 minutes

Servings: 4

Ingredients

- stevia (Optional)- 2 tbsp. (30 g)
- lemon zest -1 tsp. (4 g)
- low-fat milk-2 cups (400 ml)
- fresh Peaches chopped -2
- nuts -⅓ cup (50 g)
- quinoa -2 cups (160 g)
- vanilla extract -½ tsp. (2 g)

Preparation

1. Milk, oats, lemon zest, and vanilla extract should all be combined in a large bowl. For eight hours, or when the quinoa has absorbed the milk, cover and refrigerate the dish.
2. Oatmeal should be combined with apricots, pine nuts, and stevia.

Nutrition Information

Calories 293, Fat 11.7g, Total Carbohydrate 37.4g, Total Sugars 8.8g, Protein 11.3g, Potassium 446mg, Sodium 57 mg

Storage: In the refrigerator for up to five days, secure the jar's lid.

Reheat: just defrost at room temperature for a few hours

5.7 Breakfast Egg Salad

Preparation: 15 minutes

Cooking time: 10 minutes

Servings: 1

Ingredients

- Rib celery, diced -1
- dried rosemary -¼ tsp. (1 g)
- olive oil -1 tbsp. (15 ml)
- minced garlic – 1 tsp. (4 g)
- spinach, torn into small pieces - 1 cup (30 g)
- egg – 1
- Crumbled feta cheese, or more to taste - 1 tbsp.(15 g)
- To taste, add salt and black pepper
- Cherry tomatoes, quartered and seeded – 5
- red pepper flakes (Optional) -¼ tsp. (1g)
- diced onion -¼ cup (28 g)

Preparation

1. A big skillet is heated up over medium heat with the oil. Combine with the salt, pepper, onion, celery, rosemary, and red pepper flakes. 4 minutes should pass while simmering for the onion to become transparent. after which add the garlic. Cook for one minute.
2. Place the egg in the centre of the skillet after pushing the onion mixture to the sides. With a wooden spoon, break the yolk, then incorporate the onion mixture. Approximately three minutes after adding the tomatoes, the egg will almost be fully cooked. Feta cheese should be added and stirred for about a minute. Include spinach. Remove from heat and toss for about 30 seconds, until somewhat wilted.

Nutrition Information

Calories 587, Fat 40.7g, Total Carbohydrate 16.6g,Total Sugars 7.7g, Protein 38.5g, Potassium 396mg, Sodium 1927 mg

Storage: Put the salad on airtight container and keep in the refrigerator for up to two days.

Reheat: just defrost at room temperature for a few hours

5.8 Banana Nut Muffins

Preparation: 05 minutes
Cooking time: 20 minutes
Servings: 12

Ingredients

- Applesauce -¼ cup -120 g
- Erythritol -¾ cup -
- baking soda -1 tsp.- 4g
- Egg whites -2
- all-purpose flour -1 cup - 120 g
- ground cinnamon -1 tsp-4 g
- baking powder -1 ¼ tsp.-5g
- whole wheat flour -½ cup – 60 g
- mashed ripe banana -1 cup – 200 g

Preparation

1. Adjust the oven's temperature to 375 F. (190 degrees C). A 12-cup muffin tin should be greased or lined with paper liners.
2. Combine the flour, erythritol, baking soda, baking powder, and cinnamon in a large container. Combine the egg whites, mashed banana, and applesauce in a separate bowl. Only fully mix the dry ingredients after adding the liquid ones. Prepared muffin tins should be 3/4 full.
3. Bake in a preheated oven for 15 to 18 minutes, or until the top springs back when lightly touched. Before tapping out the muffins, let them partially cool in the pan over a wire rack.

Nutrition Information

Calories 80, Fat 0.3g, Total Carbohydrate 32.1g, Total Sugars 17.9g, Protein 2.7g, Potassium 164 mg, Sodium 111 mg

Storage: To keep muffins fresh for up to 4 days, line a zip-top bag or airtight container with paper towels and arrange the muffins in a single layer.

Reheat: just defrost at room temperature for a few hours

5.9 Quinoa Breakfast Cereal

Preparation: 05 minutes
Cooking time: 20 minutes
Servings: 4

Ingredients

- quinoa, rinsed – 1 cup (170 g)
- ground cinnamon -1 tsp. (4 g)
- chopped dried apricots -½ cup (77 g)
- Water -2 cups (480 ml)
- slivered almonds -½ cup (54 g)
- ground nutmeg -½ tsp. (2g)
- flax seeds -⅓ cup (50 g)

Preparation

1. In a skillet over medium heat, bring water and quinoa to a boil. After lowering heat, simmer for 8 to 12 minutes or until the majority of the water has been absorbed. Add the apricots, almonds, flax seeds, cinnamon, and nutmeg once the quinoa has finished cooking. Simmer for a further two to three minutes.

Nutrition Information

Calories 287, Fat 11.7g, Total Carbohydrate 35.2g, Total Sugars 2.5g, Protein 10.5g, Potassium 457mg, Sodium 9 mg

Storage: In the refrigerator for up to five days, secure the jar's lid.

Reheat: just defrost at room temperature for a few hours

5.10 Breakfast Cereal

Preparation: 15 minutes

Cooking time: 15 minutes

Servings: 12

Ingredients

- cornmeal -½ cup (60 g)
- flax seeds -½ cup (75 g)
- amaranth -½ cup (100g)
- brown basmati rice - 1 cup (185 g)
- buckwheat groats -½ cup (60 g)
- sesame seeds -½ cup (72 g)
- quinoa -½ cup (42g)
- millet -½ cup (100 g)

Preparation

1. Use a coffee grinder to grind the basmati rice into a rough powder. Fill a basin with ground rice. Quinoa, millet, buckwheat, sesame seeds, and flax seeds should all be used in the same manner.
2. Add the amaranth and cornmeal by stirring. Until you are ready to cook, Keep in the refrigerator in an airtight container.

Nutrition Information

Calories 238, Fat 6.2g , Total Carbohydrate 38.5g, Total Sugars 0.4g, Protein 7.2g, Potassium 213mg, Sodium 8 mg

Storage: In the refrigerator for up to five days, secure the jar's lid.

Reheat: just defrost at room temperature for a few hours

5.11 Poached Eggs

Preparation: 05 minutes

Cooking time: 10 minutes

Servings: 4

Ingredients

- black pepper, freshly ground, and salt as desired
- dried dill, or to taste -1 pinch
- Eggs -4
- white vinegar -2 tsp. (4 g)

Preparation

1. Fill a big pot with water until it is 2 to 3 inches deep, then heat to a simmer. Add the vinegar, turn the heat down to medium-low, and maintain a gently simmer over the water.
2. A cracked egg is placed in a small cup. Place the egg in the cup with the boiling water's surface facing up.
3. Keep utilizing the excess eggs. After the heat has been turned off and the pan is covered, the eggs should sit for 4 minutes. With a slotted spoon, remove the eggs from the pan. Add dill, pepper, and salt for seasoning.

Nutrition Information

Calories 64, Fat 4.4 g, Total Carbohydrate 0.4 g, Total Sugars 0.4 g, Protein 5.6 g, Potassium 62mg, Sodium 62 mg

Storage: Just put the egg bowl within the fridge. up to two days.

Reheat: just defrost at room temperature for a few hours

5.12 Multigrain Chia Waffles

Preparation: 15 minutes

Cooking time: 20 minutes

Servings: 8

Ingredients

- baking powder -4 tsp. (16 g)
- chia seeds -2 tbsp.(30 g)
- stevia, or more to taste -2 tsp. (8 g)
- unsweetened applesauce -½ cup (122 g)
- flax seed meal -¼ cup (38 g)
- Egg, beaten -1
- vanilla extract -1 tsp .(4 g)
- almond milk -1 ¾ cups (420 ml)
- rolled oats -½ cup (40 g)
- salt (Optional) -¼ tsp. (1g)
- whole wheat flour -1 ¼ cups (160 g)
- cooking spray

Preparation

1. Waffle irons should be preheated in accordance with the manufacturer's

recommendations; cooking spray should be applied inside.

2. Combine in a dish by whisking the almond milk, applesauce, egg, chia seeds, and vanilla extract. Wait two minutes, or until the chia seeds begin to thicken the mixture.

3. Mix the almond milk mixture with the To get a smooth batter, combine flour, oats, flax seed meal, baking powder, stevia, and salt.

4. Fill the waffle maker with 1/2 cup batter, then bake each waffle for five minutes, or until golden and crisp. Use the leftover batter to repeat.

Nutrition Information

Calories 264, Fat 15.9g, Total Carbohydrate 26.5g, Total Sugars 3.6g, Protein 6g, Potassium 478mg, Sodium 94 mg

Storage: Waffles should be placed in an airtight jar and kept in the refrigerator for at least five days.

Reheat: just defrost at room temperature for a few hours

5.13 French Toast with Blackberry Compote

Preparation: 15 minutes

Cooking time: 10 minutes

Servings: 5

Ingredients

- ground ginger -¼ tsp. (1g)
- egg, separated -1
- fresh blackberries -2 (6 ounce) containers (340 g)
- egg white -1
- ground nutmeg -¼ tsp. (1g)
- whole-grain bread -5 slices
- honey (Optional) -1 tbsp. (15 g)
- ground cinnamon -¼ tsp. (1g)

Preparation

1. 1. To make the pulpy and juicy blackberries, crush half of the blackberries in a basin. The remaining

blackberries ought should be in the tiny pot at this point. Warm up the food for 3 to 5 minutes at low heat. the compote that contains honey.

2. 2. Combine the egg whites, nutmeg, cinnamon, and ginger in a bowl with the egg yolk. It is recommended that you dip each slice of bread in the mixture for 10 to 15 seconds on each side.

3. Turn on a skillet's medium heat. Slices of the sopped bread should be browned for three minutes on each side. On top, spoon the warm berry compote.

Nutrition Information

Calories 128, Fat 2.2 g, Total Carbohydrate 21.9g, Total Sugars 8.5g, Protein 6.4g, Potassium 207mg, Sodium 152 mg

Storage: In the refrigerator for up to five days, secure the jar's lid.

Reheat: just defrost at room temperature for a few hours

5.14 Coconut Muffins

Preparation: 15 minutes

Cooking time: 20 minutes

Servings: 12

Ingredients

- baking powder -2 tsp. (8g)
- sweetened flaked coconut -¼ cup (20 g)
- Erythritol-⅓ cup (65 g)
- coconut extract -¼ tsp. (1g)
- vegetable oil -¼ cup (55 g)
- all-purpose flour -2 cups (250 g)
- salt -¼ tsp. (1 g)
- large egg, lightly beaten -1
- Cooking spray
- large egg white, lightly beaten -1
- vanilla yogurt -1 (8 ounce) container (226 g)

Preparation

1. Increase the oven's setting to 400 F. (200 degrees C). Spray 12 muffin pans with cooking oil.
2. Combine the flour, erythritol, coconut, baking soda, and salt in a sizable bowl. In the centre of the mixture, make a well. Combine the yoghurt, egg, egg white, vegetable oil, and coconut essence completely in a separate bowl. Whisk the egg mixture before adding it to the bowl containing the dry ingredients. Each muffin cup should hold 3/4 cup of batter.
3. Bake for roughly 20 minutes, or until just beginning to brown., in the preheated oven. The muffins should be removed from the pan as soon as possible.

Nutrition Information

Calories 165, Fat 5.9g , Total Carbohydrate 23.5g, Total Sugars 7.1g, Protein 4.1g, Potassium 167 mg, Sodium 74 mg

Storage: Place the muffins in a single layer and line a zip-top bag or airtight box with paper towels to keep them fresh for up to 4 days.

Reheat: just defrost at room temperature for a few hours

5.15 Avocado-Egg Toast

Preparation: 10 minutes

Cooking time: 00 minutes

Servings: 1

Ingredients

- scallion, sliced (Optional) -1 tbsp. (15 g)
- garlic powder – pinch of
- large egg, fried -1
- whole-wheat bread, toasted -1 slice
- Avocado -¼
- Sriracha (Optional) -1 tsp. (4g)
- ground pepper -¼ tsp. (1 g)

Preparation

1. In a small bowl, mix the avocado, pepper, and garlic powder. Carefully mash.
2. Place a fried egg on top of the toast along with the avocado mixture. If desired, garnish with scallion and Sriracha.

Nutrition Information

Calories 261, Fat 15.8 g, Total Carbohydrate 20.1g, Total Sugars 3g ,Protein 11.5g, Potassium 434 mg, Sodium 242 mg

Storage: Put the salad on airtight container Keep in the refrigerator for up to five days.

Reheat: just defrost at room temperature for a few hours

6   SALADS RECIPES

6.1   Chicken Salad

Preparation: 05 minutes

Cooking time: 30 minutes

Servings: 6

Ingredients

Baked chicken

- boneless skinless chicken thighs -2 lbs.
- onion powder -½ tsp.(2 g)
- Pepper -½ tsp.(2 g)
- Olive oil spray

- garlic powder -½ tsp.(2 g)
- salt -½ tsp.(2 g)

Salad

- tomato, diced -1
- pomegranate seeds -¼ cup (35 g)
- small stalk of fennel, sliced thinly (divided) -1
- kale, chopped in bite-sized pieces -3 cups (90 g)
- red onion, sliced thinly -1

- Brussel sprouts, chopped into bite-sized slices -1 cup (88 g)
- purple cabbage, sliced -1 cup (70 g)
- carrot, cut in ribbons with a mandolin (or sliced thinly) -1
- cucumber, chopped in bite-sized pieces -1
- crumbled feta (optional) -¼ cup (38 g)

Garlic Citrus Vinaigrette

- extra virgin olive oil -¼ cup (60 ml)
- lemons, juiced (approximately 4 tbsp. juice) –(60 ml)
- salt -½ tsp. (2 g)
- minced fennel (reserved from above) – 1tsp. (4 g)
- pepper -½ tsp. (2 g)
- Garlic cloves, minced -1

Preparation

1. A 375°F (190°C) oven should be ready. The chicken thighs are seasoned on both sides before going into a small pan that has been oiled with olive.
2. Put in the oven for 30 minutes, or until the internal thigh temperature reaches 165 degrees, whichever comes first. Set aside and allow to cool.
3. While the chicken bakes, prepare the salad's ingredients. Chop the Brussels sprouts, cucumber, and kale. Red onion, fennel, purple cabbage, and carrot all need to be thinly sliced. Dissect the tomato. The ingredients should be combined in a sizable basin, then chilled until used.
4. In a mason jar, combine all the vinaigrette ingredients and give it a good shake. Put in the fridge until required.
5. Chop the chicken into bite-sized pieces after it has cooled, then serve it over salad. Add vinaigrette and stir after.

Nutrition Information
Calories 329, Fat 16.6 g, Total Carbohydrate 14.7g, Total Sugars 5.2g, Protein 30.6g, Potassium 675 mg, Sodium 415 mg
Storage: Simply keep in the refrigerator in little, sealed containers to enjoy over the course of the week.
Reheat: just defrost at room temperature for a few hours

6.2 Cobb salad

Preparation: 05 minutes
Cooking time: 00 minutes
Servings: 1

Ingredients

- mixed green salad -2 cups – (56 g)
- feta cheese, -1 oz. (28 g)
- avocado -½
- cherry tomatoes -4
- hard boiled egg -1
- cooked bacon, crumbled -¼ cup (30 g)
- feta cheese, -1 oz. (28 g)

Preparation

1. Avocado and tomatoes should be diced. Cut the boiled egg into slices.
2. Put the mixed greens on a big dish or salad bowl.
3. The feta cheese, bacon bits, and diced chicken breast should all be measured out.
4. On top of the greens, arrange tomatoes, avocados, eggs, chicken, feta, and bacon in horizontal rows.

Nutrition Information

Calories 412, Fat 23.6 g, Total Carbohydrate 11.9 g , Total Sugars 2.9g, Protein 38.4g, Potassium 543 mg, Sodium 914 mg
Storage: For three to four days, keep them in the refrigerator in a sealed container.
Reheat: just defrost at room temperature for a few hours

6.3 Blackberry Balsamic Spinach Salad

Preparation: 10 minutes
Cooking time: 00 minutes
Servings: 6

Ingredients

- green onions, thinly sliced -2
- chopped walnuts, toasted -1/4 cup (32 g)
- fresh blackberries, halved -2 cups (290 g)
- cherry tomatoes, halved -1-1/2 cups (270 g)
- crumbled feta cheese -1/3 cup (50 g)
- balsamic vinaigrette -1/3 cup (10 ml)
- fresh baby spinach -3 cups (90 g)

Preparation

1. Combine the first six ingredients in a large bowl. After dividing the salad among the six bowls, drizzle the dressing on top.

Nutrition Information

Calories 139, Fat 11.5 g, Total Carbohydrate 8.4g, Total Sugars 4.6g, Protein 3.9g, Potassium 279 mg, Sodium 214 mg

Storage: The salad can be kept in the refrigerator for at least five days if it is placed in an airtight container.

Reheat: just defrost at room temperature for a few hours

6.4 Tuna Nicoise Salad

Preparation: 10 minutes
Cooking time: 05 minutes
Servings: 1

Ingredients

- cucumber -3½ oz. (100 g)
- Radish – 1
- balsamic vinegar -1 tsp. (4 g)
- pepper-½ tsp. (2g)
- baby spinach - 3 oz. (85 g)
- Dijon mustard -½ tsp. (2g)
- whole egg – 1
- red bell pepper -½
- green beans -2 oz. (55) g
- ahi tuna steak -4 oz. (115 g)
- large black olives – 3
- olive oil - 1 tsp. (4 g)
- Handful of parsley
- broccoli -1½ oz. (40 g)

Preparation

1. The egg should be boiled and then let to cool.
2. Set aside the beans and broccoli after they have been cooked. It merely takes a few minutes in the microwave or a pot of boiling water.
3. Heat a little oil in a pan over high heat. Before being placed to the pan and fried for 2 minutes on each side, the tuna needs to be peppered all over. Add the spinach to your entrée or salad bowl.
4. Bell pepper, cucumber, and egg should all be chopped into bite-sized pieces. Add to the spinach's top.
5. Slice the radish and combine it with the beans, broccoli, and olives. Add to the spinach salad on top.
6. Include the tuna slices in the salad.
7. In a bowl, mix the salt, pepper, balsamic vinegar, mustard, and olive oil.
8. After you've finished, add the chopped parsley.
9. Spoon the vinaigrette over the salad using a spoon.

Nutrition Information

Calories 405, Fat 13.1 g, Total Carbohydrate 18.4g, Total Sugars 8.4g, Protein 39 g, Potassium 1250 mg, Sodium 586 mg

Storage: The salad can be kept in the refrigerator for at least five days if it is placed in an airtight container.

Reheat: just defrost at room temperature for a few hours

6.5 Cherry Tomato Salad

Preparation: 15 minutes

Cooking time: 00 minutes

Servings: 6

Ingredients

- minced fresh oregano -1 to 2 tsp. (4 -8 g)
- salt -1/2 tsp. ((2 g)
- minced fresh parsley -1/4 cup (15 g)
- Erythritol -1/2 tsp. (2 g)
- cherry tomatoes, halved -1 quart (950 g)
- minced fresh basil -1 to 2 tsp. (4 -8 g)
- white vinegar -3 tbsp. (45 ml)
- canola oil -1/4 cup (55 g)

Preparation

1. In a small bowl, place the tomatoes. Oil, vinegar, salt, and erythritol should all be combined in a small dish before adding the herbs. To uniformly coat the tomatoes, pour over and toss. Overnight, covered, in the refrigerator.

Nutrition Information

Calories 106, Fat 9.4 g, Total Carbohydrate 5.4g, Total Sugars 3.6g, Protein 1.5g, Potassium 308 mg, Sodium 201 mg

Storage: The salad can be kept in the refrigerator for at least five days if it is placed in an airtight container.

Reheat: just defrost at room temperature for a few hours

6.6 Hot Spinach Apple Salad

Preparation: 10 minutes

Cooking time: 00 minutes

Servings: 10

Ingredients

- fresh baby spinach -9 cups (270 g)
- red apples, thinly sliced -2
- brown sugar -3 tbsp. – (45 g)
- bacon strips, diced -6
- red onion, chopped -1
- cider vinegar -1/4 cup 60 ml

Preparation

1. Cook bacon until it is crisp in a big skillet. to paper towels, remove. Save 2 tsp. of the drippings after draining.
2. Combine vinegar, brown sugar, and any saved drippings in the same skillet. Once it starts to boil, heat and stir it until the sugar dissolves. Cool a little.
3. In the meantime, put the spinach, apples, onion, and bacon in a serving bowl. Put on a coat and pour on a warm dressing. Serve immediately.

Nutrition Information

Calories 100, Fat 5.5 g, Total Carbohydrate 9.5g, Total Sugars 6.2 g, Protein 3.3g, Potassium 204 mg, Sodium 203 mg

Storage: The salad can be kept in the refrigerator for at least five days if it is placed in an airtight container.

Reheat: just defrost at room temperature for a few hours

6.7 Watermelon and Spinach Salad

Preparation: 30 minutes

Cooking time: 00 minutes

Servings: 8

Ingredients

- Erythritol -1/4 tsp. (1 g)
- lime juice -2 tbsp. (30 ml)
- pepper -1/4 tsp. (1 g)
- minced fresh gingerroot -4 tsp. (16 g)
- garlic cloves, minced -2
- grated lime zest -1 tbsp. (15 g)
- rice vinegar or white wine vinegar -1/4 cup (60 ml)
- canola oil -2 tbsp. (30 ml)
- salt -1/2 tsp. (2 g)

Salad:

- Green onions chopped -2
- cubed English cucumber -2 cups (200 g)
- cubed cantaloupe -2 cups (150 g)

- cubed seedless watermelon -3 cups (840 g)
- chopped fresh cilantro -1/2 cup (2 g)
- fresh baby spinach or arugula - 4 cups (120 g)

Preparation

1. Whisk the first nine ingredients in a small dish. Salad ingredients should be combined in a big bowl. Serve right away after drizzling on dressing and tossing to combine.

Nutrition Information

Calories 76, Fat 3.7 g , Total Carbohydrate 9.5g, Total Sugars 6.4g , Protein 1.5g, Potassium 141 mg, Sodium 157 mg

Storage: The salad can be kept in the refrigerator for at least five days if it is placed in an airtight container.

Reheat: just defrost at room temperature for a few hours

6.8 Marinated Beet Salad

Preparation: 10 minutes

Cooking time: 10 minutes

Servings: 4

Ingredients

- whole beets -1 (16 ounce) can (450 g)
- prepared mustard -1 tsp. (4 g)
- stevia -¼ cup (10 g)
- white wine vinegar -¼ cup (60 ml)
- diced red onion -¼ cup (30 g)

Preparation

1. After 1/4 cup of the liquid has been collected, the beets should be rinsed and cut into 1/4 to 1/2 inch slivers. Omit the onions.
2. Over medium heat, stir the stevia, 1/4 cup liquid, and mustard until the stevia has completely dissolved. The vinegar should be heated until it boils, then it should be allowed to cool.
3. Combine the ingredients and chill for 4 to 6 hours after adding the mixture to the onion and beet slices. Serve at room

temperature after taking it out of the fridge.

Nutrition Information

Calories 89, Fat 0.1 g, Total Carbohydrate 20.5g, Total Sugars 5.2 g, Protein 0.1g, Potassium 23mg, Sodium 245 mg

Storage: The salad can be kept in the refrigerator for at least five days if it is placed in an airtight container.

Reheat: just defrost at room temperature for a few hours

6.9 Sweet Carrot Salad

Preparation: 10 minutes

Cooking time: 30 minutes

Servings: 8

Ingredients

- crushed pineapple -1 cup (165 g)
- lemon juice -1 dash
- carrots, grated -1 pound (450 g)
- honey -1 tbsp. (15 g)
- mayonnaise, or to taste -2 tbsp. (30 g)
- raisins -½ cup (75 g)
-

Preparation

1. Combine the raisins, pineapple, and carrots in a big container. Add the honey, mayonnaise, and lemon juice, then combine. To give the flavours time to combine, 30 minutes or more before serving, put in the refrigerator.

Nutrition Information

Calories 91, Fat 2.6 g , Total Carbohydrate 17.6g, Total Sugars 12.3g, Protein 0.9g, Potassium 273 mg, Sodium 60 mg

Storage: The salad can be kept in the refrigerator for at least five days if it is placed in an airtight container.

Reheat: just defrost at room temperature for a few hours

6.10 Ruby Raspberry Slaw

Preparation: 10 minutes

Cooking time: 00 minutes

Servings: 6

Ingredients

- prepared raspberry vinaigrette -1/4 cup (60 ml)
- mayonnaise -3 tbsp. (45 g)
- shredded carrots -1 cup (125 g)
- shredded red cabbage -2 cups (140 g)
- fresh raspberries -1/2 cup (62 g)
- shredded cabbage -2 cups (140 g)
- pepper -1/4 tsp. (1 g)

Preparation

1. In a large bowl, combine the cabbage and carrots. In a small bowl, mix the vinaigrette, pepper, and mayonnaise. Combine with the cabbage mixture after adding. 10 minutes in a refrigerator covered. On top, add raspberries.

Nutrition Information

Calories 108, Fat 7.2 g, Total Carbohydrate 10.2g, Total Sugars 6.6g, Protein 1g, Potassium 116 mg, Sodium 106 mg

Storage The salad can be kept in the refrigerator for at least five days if it is placed in an airtight container.

Reheat: just defrost at room temperature for a few hours

6.11 Cucumber and Carrot Salad

Preparation: 10 minutes

Cooking time: 00 minutes

Servings: 4

Ingredients

- chili powder -1 tsp. (4 g)
- Cucumber, sliced -1
- lime, juiced -1
- pinch of cayenne pepper, or more to taste
- baby carrots -1 (8 ounce) package (230 g)
- salt -¼ tsp. (1 g)

Preparation

1. Cucumber, baby carrots, lime juice, chilli powder, salt, and cayenne pepper should all be combined in a bowl and stirred to blend well.

Nutrition Information

Calories 38, Fat 0.3 g , Total Carbohydrate 9.5g, Total Sugars 4.3g , Protein 1.1g, Potassium 275 mg, Sodium 200 mg

Storage: The salad can be kept in the refrigerator for at least five days if it is placed in an airtight container.

Reheat: just defrost at room temperature for a few hours

6.12 Broccoli and Apple Salad

Preparation: 15 minutes

Cooking time: 00 minutes

Servings: 6

Ingredients

- red onion -1 tbsp. (10 g)
- Bacon strips, cooked and crumbled -4
- red onion -1 tbsp. (10 g)
- reduced-fat plain yogurt -1/2 cup (88 g)
- mixed dried fruit -1/2 cup (100g)
- fresh broccoli florets -3 cups (210 g)

Preparation

1. Combine the broccoli, apples, dried fruit, and onion in a medium bowl. Yogurt is blended after. Bacon is a must. Keep chilled until serving.

Nutrition Information

Calories 202, Fat 6.5 g, Total Carbohydrate 34.1g, Total Sugars 3g, Protein 5.3g, Potassium 467 mg, Sodium 226 mg

Storage: The salad can be kept in the refrigerator for at least five days if it is placed in an airtight container.

Reheat: just defrost at room temperature for a few hours

6.13 Corn and Green Pepper Salad

Preparation: 20 minutes

Cooking time: 00 minutes

Servings: 2

Ingredients

- finely chopped green pepper -¼ cup (35 g)
- fresh corn in the husk -2 ears
- stevia -1 tsp. (4 g)
- chopped hot green chile peppers -3 tbsp. (45 g)
- ground cumin -½ tsp. (2g)
- white vinegar -2 tbsp. (30 ml)
- freshly ground black pepper to taste

Preparation

1. Use a big, sharp knife to trim the corn stalk to about 1/2 inch. Corn should not be shucked.
2. Ice and cold water should be added to a big dish.
3. 2 minutes each ear of corn on high in the microwave. Remove the silk and husks with care. Corn should be thrown into the icy water. Corn should be drained and pat dried.
4. Slice kernels off corn while holding it erect and rotating the ear as you work. Transfer kernels to a bowl and stir in vinegar, stevia, cumin, green pepper, and green chile peppers. Until serving, chill.

Nutrition Information

Calories 151,Fat 1.8 g, Total Carbohydrate 34.5g, Total Sugars 8.1g, Protein 4.5g, Potassium 263 mg, Sodium 576mg

Storage: The salad can be kept in the refrigerator for at least five days if it is placed in an airtig ht container.

Reheat: just defrost at room temperature for a few hours

6.14 Sour Cream Cucumbers

Preparation: 15 minutes

Cooking time: 00 minutes

Servings: 8

Ingredients

- stevia -1 tbsp. (15 g)
- sour cream -1/2 cup (115 g)
- sweet onion, thinly sliced and separated into rings -1 small
- Pepper to taste
- cucumbers, peeled, if desired, and thinly sliced -4 medium
- white vinegar -3 tbsp. (45 ml)

Preparation

1. The following ingredients should be carefully combined in a large bowl: sour cream, vinegar, stevia, and pepper. Toss in the onion and cucumbers after adding them. Refrigerate for at least 4 hours while covered. Use a slotted spoon just before serving.

Nutrition Information

Calories 64, Fat 3.2 g, Total Carbohydrate 8.5g, Total Sugars 4.4g, Protein 1.5g, Potassium 259 mg, Sodium 11 mg

Storage: The salad can be kept in the refrigerator for at least five days if it is placed in an airtight container.

Reheat: just defrost at room temperature for a few hours

6.15 Quinoa Tabbouleh

Preparation: 10 minutes

Cooking time: 00 minutes

Servings: 8

Ingredients

- pepper -1/2 tsp. (2g)
- minced fresh parsley -1/3 cup (20 g)
- olive oil -2 tbsp. (30 ml)
- salt -1/2 tsp. (2 g)
- quinoa, rinsed -1 cup (170 g)
- Water -2 cups (480 ml)
- lemon juice -1/4 cup (60 ml)

- rinsed and drained black beans, -1 can (15 ounces) (425 g)
- cucumber, peeled and chopped -1 small
- sweet red pepper, chopped -1 small

Preparation

1. In a large saucepan, bring water to a rolling boil. is quinoa. Cook for 12 to 15 minutes with the lid on, or until the liquid is completely absorbed. Use a fork to fluff the meal after removing it from the heat. Place in a basin and allow to totally cool.
2. Include the parsley, red pepper, cucumber, and beans. In a small bowl, mix the remaining ingredients. After adding the ingredients, toss the salad to combine them. Keep chilled in the fridge.

Nutrition Information

Calories 204, Fat 5.8 g, Total Carbohydrate 31.7g, Total Sugars 2.1g, Protein 8.8g, Potassium 588 mg, Sodium 156 mg

Storage: The salad can be kept in the refrigerator for at least five days if it is placed in an airtight container.

Reheat: just defrost at room temperature for a few hours

7 SOUP RECIPES

7.1 Lentil-Tomato Soup

Preparation: 15 minutes
Cooking time: 30 minutes
Servings: 6

Ingredients

- tomato paste -1 can (6 ounces) – 170 g
- pepper -1/4 tsp. – 1 g
- dill weed -1/4 tsp. – 1 g
- dried brown lentils, rinsed -2/3 cup - 34 g
- dried thyme -1/2 tsp. 2 g
- brown sugar -1 tbsp- 15 g
- onion, chopped -1 medium
- minced fresh parsley -2 tbsp. – 30 g
- carrots, sliced -4 medium
- garlic salt -1 tsp. – 4 g
- dried tarragon -1/4 tsp. – 1 g
- Water -4-1/2 cups – 1.8 L
- white vinegar -1 tbsp. – 15 ml

Preparation

1. Heat the water, lentils, carrots, and onion to a boil in a big pot. For 20 to 25 minutes, reduce the heat, cover the pan, and simmer the vegetables and lentils. Add the last few ingredients, mix, and bring to a boil once more. To enable flavours to meld, lower heat and simmer, uncovered, for 5 minutes.

Nutrition Information

Calories 73, Fat 0.2 g, Total Carbohydrate 15.9g, Total Sugars 7.8g , Protein 3.1g, Potassium 466 mg, Sodium 63 mg

Storage:a sealed container is used to store soup for up to 3 -4 days.

Reheat: just defrost at room temperature for a few hours

7.2 Roasted Cauliflower & Red Pepper Soup

Preparation: 50 minutes
Cooking time: 25 minutes
Servings: 6

Ingredients

- 2% milk -1 cup – 240 ml
- cayenne pepper - 1/4 tsp. 1 g
- minced fresh rosemary -2-1/2 tsp – 10 g
- Garlic cloves, minced – 2
- sweet red peppers, halved and seeded - 2 medium
- Salt -1/2 tsp. – 2 g
- Pepper -1/4 tsp. 1 g
- olive oil, divided -4 tbsp. 60 ml

- all-purpose flour -1/4 cup
- paprika -1/2 tsp. – 2 g
- chopped sweet onion -1 cup -115g
- Shredded Parmesan cheese, optional
- chicken stock -4 cups – 960 ml
- cauliflower, broken into florets -1 large

Preparation

1. The broiler should be turned on. Peppers should be placed skin-side up on a foil-lined baking sheet. Broil the vegetables 4 inches from the heat for about 5 minutes, or until the skins are blistered. Cover the bowl after the transfer and let it to stand for 20 minutes. Heat the oven to 400 degrees on the bake setting.
2. After tossing the cauliflower with 2 tablespoons of oil, spread it out in a 15x10x1-inch pan. Roast until soft for 25 to 30 minutes, stirring once halfway through. Before being cut, peppers need to be cleaned and seeded.
3. In a 6-quart stockpot, heat the remaining 2 tablespoons of oil to medium-low. When the onion is yellow and ready to be added, do so. Cook while stirring for 6 to 8 minutes. The rosemary, paprika, and garlic should be heated and stirred for one minute. After thoroughly combining the flour, boil for a minute while stirring. Stock is gently stirred in. Bring to a boil while stirring constantly, then simmer while stirring constantly until thickened.
4. Combine the cauliflower and peppers. Pour the soup into an immersion blender and purée it. Alternately, let the soup to cool somewhat and then mix it in portions. Heat the milk and the remaining ingredients completely. If preferred, top the food with Parmesan.

Nutrition Information

Calories 184, Fat 10.9 g, Total Carbohydrate 19.2g, Total Sugars 8.5g,Protein 5.8g, Potassium 576 mg, Sodium 766mg

Storage: a sealed container is used to store soup for up to 3 -4 days
Reheat: just defrost at room temperature for a few hours

7.3 Tomato Soup

Preparation: 15 minutes
Cooking time: 15 minutes
Servings: 4

Ingredients

- finely chopped celery -1/4 cup - 25 g
- brown sugar -2 tsp. – 8 g
- salt -1/2 tsp. 2 g
- diced tomatoes, undrained -2 cans (14-1/2 ounces each) – 850 g
- finely chopped onion -1/4 cup -28 g
- canola oil - 2 tsp- 8ml
- coarsely ground pepper -1/4 tsp. 1g
- dried basil -1/2 tsp. 2 g
- Minced fresh basil, optional
- water -1-1/2 cups – 480 ml
- dried oregano -1/4 tsp. 1 g

Preparation

1. An enormous pan of oil needs to be heated to a medium-high temperature. The onion and celery should be sautéed and combined for 2-4 minutes, or until tender. If preferred, eliminate the fresh basil before adding the remaining ingredients. boiling point To allow flavours to merge, lower heat, cover, and simmer for ten minutes.
2. Puree the soup using an immersion blender. Instead, you might slightly cool the soup and combine it in batches. In the pan, cook it once more. You can top the dish with some freshly minced basil if you wish.

Nutrition Information

Calories 69, Fat 2.8g, Total Carbohydrate 10.7g, Total Sugars 7.4g, Protein 2g, Potassium 535 mg, Sodium 309 mg
Stoage : a sealed container is used to store soup for up to 3 -4 days

Reheat: just defrost at room temperature for a few hours

7.4 Dill Chicken Soup

Preparation: 15 minutes
Cooking time: 20 minutes
Servings: 6

Ingredients

- coarsely shredded rotisserie chicken -1-1/2 cups -126 g
- reduced-sodium chicken broth -6 cups – 1.4 L
- onion, coarsely chopped -1 small
- chopped fresh dill -2 tbsp.- 30 g
- Garlic cloves, minced -2
- uncooked whole wheat orzo pasta -1/2 cup -42 g
- carrots, chopped -2 medium
- frozen peas (about 6 ounces) -1-1/2 cups -170 g
- Coarsely ground pepper, optional
- fresh baby spinach (about 10 cups) -8 ounces -225 g
- lemon juice -2 tbsp.- 30 g
- canola oil -1 tbsp. 15 ml

Preparation

1. In a 6-qt stockpot, warm the oil over moderate heat. Cook the carrots, onion, and garlic for a further 4-5 minutes, or until the carrots are soft.
2. Stir in the orzo, chicken, and broth. Simmer for five minutes, then lower the heat and cover the pan. Add the peas, spinach, and dill, then bring back to a boil. To cook orzo, cover the pan and boil for three to four minutes, or until tender. Blend in lemon juice. If you'd like, garnish each plate with some freshly ground pepper.

Nutrition Information

Calories 157, Fat 5.9 g, Total Carbohydrate 14.8g, Total Sugars 4g , Protein 11g, Potassium 556 mg, Sodium 885 mg

Storage: a sealed container is used to store soup for up to 3 -4 days
Reheat: just defrost at room temperature for a few hours

7.5 Cream of Wild Rice Soup

Preparation: 15 minutes
Cooking time: 20 minutes
Servings: 10

Ingredients

- cubed cooked chicken breast -1 cup -140 g
- butter -1/4 cup – 56 g
- reduced-sodium chicken broth -8 cups – 2 L
- pepper -1/4 tsp. – 1g
- all-purpose flour -1/2 cup -62 g
- carrot, shredded -1 large
- fat-free evaporated milk -1 cup – 240 ml
- cooked wild rice -3 cups -480 g
- chives -1/4 cup – 3g
- celery rib, -1
- salt -1/4 tsp. 1 g
- onion, chopped -1 large

Preparation

1. In a pan over medium heat, cook the celery, onion, and carrot until soft. Mix well after adding the flour. Add the broth little by little. Rice, chicken, and pepper are all mixed together. Over medium heat, bring to a boil. After two minutes, or until thickened, simmer and stir. Add the milk and continue cooking for an additional 3 to 5 minutes. Sprinkle chives on top.

Nutrition Information

Calories 331, Fat 8.7 g, Total Carbohydrate 46.5g, Total Sugars 5.4g, Protein 17.5g, Potassium 546 mg, Sodium 751 mg
Storage:a sealed container is used to store soup for up to 3 -4 days
Reheat: just defrost at room temperature for a few hours

7.6 Asparagus Soup

Preparation: 20 minutes

Cooking time: 55 minutes

Servings: 12

Ingredients

- dried thyme -1/4 tsp. 1 g
- olive oil -1 tbsp. 15 ml
- carrot, thinly sliced -1
- uncooked long grain brown rice -2/3 cup – 126 g
- Salt -1/2 tsp . 2g
- butter -1 tbsp. 15 g
- Pepper -1/4 tsp. 1 g
- chicken broth -6 cups – 1.4 L
- fresh asparagus, -2 pounds- 900 g
- onion, - 1

Preparation

1. In a 6-qt stockpot set over medium heat, melt the butter and oil. When the veggies are done, add the seasonings, and stir frequently for 8 to 10 minutes.
2. When the liquid is at a boil, add the rice. Cook rice for 40–45 minutes, stirring periodically, under cover, or until tender.
3. Purée the soup with an immersion blender or combine it in small batches after letting it cool slightly. Reheat the meal in the pot all the way. If you want, you can garnish with croutons and sour cream.

Nutrition Information

Calories 97, Fat 3.2 g , Total Carbohydrate 12.8g, Total Sugars 2.4g, Protein 5g, Potassium 315 mg, Sodium 491 mg

Storage:a sealed container is used to store soup for up to 3 -4 days

Reheat: just defrost at room temperature for a few hours

7.7 Creamy Chicken Rice Soup

Preparation: 15 minutes

Cooking time: 15 minutes

Servings: 4

Ingredients

- carrot, chopped – 1
- chicken broth -2 cans (14-1/2 ounces each) – 800 ml
- Celery rib, chopped – 1
- all-purpose flour -3 tbsp.- 45 g
- cubed cooked chicken breast -2 cups - 280 g
- pepper -1/4 tsp. – 1 g
- Onion -1/2 cup
- uncooked long grain rice -1/3 cup – 60 g
- Garlic -1/2 tsp. – 2 g
- evaporated milk -1 can (5 ounces) 140ml
- dried basil -3/4 tsp.-3 g
- canola oil -1 tbsp – 15 ml

Preparation

1. Heat the oil in a large pot over medium heat before adding the celery, onion, and carrot to sauté. After adding the garlic, stir for a minute. Stirring while bringing the stock, rice, and spices to a boil Rice should be cooked for 15 minutes, covered, until soft.
2. After the flour and milk have been fully incorporated, stir the soup. Bring to a boil, then simmer for two minutes while stirring periodically to thicken. Add the chicken and heat it through.

Nutrition Information

Calories   400

Fat 14.5 g

Total Carbohydrate 30.5g

Total Sugars 11.4g

Protein 34.5g

Potassium 789 mg

Sodium 115 mg

Storage:a sealed container is used to store soup for up to 3 -4 days

Reheat: just defrost at room temperature for a few hours

7.8 Turkey and Vegetable Barley Soup

Preparation: 15 minutes

Cooking time: 10 minutes

Servings: 6

Ingredients

- cubed cooked turkey breast -2 cups – 56 g
- onion, chopped – 1
- Pepper -1/2 tsp. 2 g
- Carrots, chopped – 5
- canola oil -1 tbsp. 15 ml
- chicken broth -6 cups – 1.4 L
- quick-cooking barley -2/3 cup – 122 g
- fresh baby spinach -2 cups – 60 g

Preparation

1. Oil should be heated to a medium-high temperature in a big pan. Add the onion and carrots after they are crisp-tender. For a further four to five minutes, simmer and stir.
2. Barley and broth are added, then the mixture is heated to a boil. Reduce the heat and cover the pot as soon as the barley and carrots are cooked through. Heat through the turkey, spinach, and pepper.

Nutrition Information

Calories 133 , Fat 4.1 g, Total Carbohydrate 16.7g, Total Sugars 4.1g, Protein 7.8g, Potassium 493 mg, Sodium 853mg

Storage: a sealed container is used to store soup for up to 3 -4 days

Reheat: just defrost at room temperature for a few hours

7.9 Broccoli Soup

Preparation: 15 minutes

Cooking time: 35 minutes

Servings: 8

Ingredients

- broccoli stalks, - 3
- cloves garlic -3 large
- broccoli florets and stalks, - 2
- low-sodium chicken stock -4 cups – 960 ml
- olive oil -1 tbsp. -15 ml
- celery root,– 1/3
- yellow onion – 1
- large potatoes, peeled and coarsely chopped -2

Preparation

1. Warm up the olive oil in a pot gradually. Add the onion and garlic when they are transparent, then boil and stir for 10 to 15 minutes. Potatoes, celery root, broccoli stems, and florets of broccoli are combined and coated in oil. The vegetables are covered with chicken stock, which has been cooked until it boils.
2. The veggies should be able to be easily punctured with a fork after 20 to 25 minutes of simmering, during which time the heat should be reduced to low. Take the soup off the heat.
3. Blender should only be half-full of fluids and veggies. After a few pulses, increase the blender's speed to its highest setting while holding the lid down. 45–1 minute should be spent pureeing the soup until it is light green and creamy. Repeat in batches with the remaining soup.

Nutrition Information

Calories 64, Fat 3.2 g , Total Carbohydrate 8.5g, Total Sugars 4.4g , Protein 1.5g, Potassium 259 mg, Sodium 11 mg

Storage: a sealed container is used to store soup for up to 3 -4 days

Reheat: just defrost at room temperature for a few hours

7.10 Bean Soup with Kale

Preparation: 15 minutes

Cooking time: 00 minutes

Servings: 8

Ingredients

- chopped raw kale -4 cups - 270 g
- Salt and pepper to taste
- dried Italian herb seasoning -2 tsp.-8 g
- white beans, -2 (15 ounce) cans -850 g
- yellow onion, chopped -1 medium
- tomatoes, - 4
- chopped parsley -1 cup – 60 g
- chicken or vegetable broth -4 cups – 960 ml
- garlic cloves, -8 large
- olive oil or canola oil -1 tbsp.- 15 ml

Preparation

1. A big pot of olive oil is becoming warm. Once added, sauté the onion and garlic until soft. Kale should be added and stir-fried until it wilts. The tomato, 3 cups of broth, 2 cups of beans, all of the herbs, salt, and pepper should be added. 5 minutes of simmering Before blending or pulsing, the remaining beans and broth should be thoroughly combined.
2. Stir in to thicken the soup. a simmer for fifteen minutes Pour into serving dishes, then sprinkle with parsley powder.

Nutrition Information

Calories 179, Fat 3.5 g, Total Carbohydrate 24.6g, Total Sugars 4.4g, Protein 10.5g, Potassium 455 mg, Sodium 822 mg

Storage:a sealed container is used to store soup for up to 3 -4 days

Reheat: just defrost at room temperature for a few hours

8   VEGETARIAN DISHES

8.1 Vegetarian Black Bean Pasta

Preparation: 15 minutes

Cooking time:20 minutes

Servings: 6

Ingredients

- fresh baby spinach - 2 cups – 60 g
- uncooked whole wheat fettuccine -9 ounces -255 g
- dried rosemary, crushed -1 tsp. – 4 g
- Garlic clove, minced – 1
- black beans, rinsed and drained -1 can (15 ounces) – 425 g
- dried oregano -1/2 tsp . 2 g
- olive oil -1 tbsp. – 15 ml
- sliced baby portobello mushrooms -1-3/4 cups – 122 g
- diced tomatoes, undrained -1 can (14-1/2 ounces) – 425 g

Preparation

1. Prepare the fettuccine in accordance with the directions on the package. A big skillet set over medium-high heat should be used to preheat the oil while waiting. The mushrooms should be stir-fried for 4-6 minutes, or until cooked through. Cook the garlic for an additional minute after adding it.
2. Stir in the tomatoes, thyme, oregano, and black beans. Add the spinach and stir until it wilts. After draining, combine the fettuccine with the bean mixture and toss.

Nutrition Information

Calories 423 , Fat 4.3 g, Total Carbohydrate 73.4g, Total Sugars 3.6g, Protein 23.3g Potassium 1317 mg, Sodium 23 mg

Storage:a sealed container is used to store Vegetarian Black Bean Pasta for up to 3 -4 days

Reheat: just defrost at room temperature for a few hours

8.2 Grilled Veggie Pizza

Preparation: 30 minutes

Cooking time: 10 minutes

Servings: 6

Ingredients

- fresh mushrooms, halved -8 small
- white wine vinegar -1 tbsp. 15 ml
- sweet red pepper, sliced -1 small
- thin whole wheat pizza crust -1 prebaked 12-inch
- tomatoes, chopped -2 small
- pizza sauce -1 can (8 ounces) -225 g
- olive oil, divided -4 tsp. -8 ml
- shredded part-skim mozzarella cheese - 2 cups – 60 g
- salt -1/4 tsp 1 g
- sweet yellow pepper, sliced -1 small
- zucchini, cut into 1/4-inch slices -1 small
- water -1 tbsp. 15 ml
- minced fresh basil -2 teaspoons – 8 g
- onion, sliced -1 small
- pizza sauce -1 can (8 ounces) -225 g
- pepper -1/4 tsp 1 g

Preparation

1. In a large bowl, combine the mushrooms, zucchini, peppers, onions, vinegar, water, three teaspoons of oil, and seasonings. Go to a wok or grill basket. When the steak is tender, cook it for 8 to 10 minutes, flipping once.
2. In step two, prepare the grill for indirect heat. Pizza sauce should be spread onto the crust before adding the last of the oil. As garnishes, include cheese, tomatoes, and grilled vegetables. Grill the dish over indirect medium heat with the lid on for 10 to 12 minutes, or until the sides are lightly browned and the cheese has melted. For a crust that is evenly browned, pizza should be turned about halfway during cooking.

Nutrition Information

Calories 117, Fat 5.6 g, Total Carbohydrate 13.6g, Total Sugars 3.2g, Protein 5.3g, Potassium 290 mg, Sodium 205mg

Storage: a sealed container is used to store Grilled Veggie Pizza for up to 3 -4 days

Reheat: just defrost at room temperature for a few hours

8.3 Black Bean-Tomato Chili

Preparation: 15 minutes
Cooking time: 35 minutes
Servings: 6

Ingredients

- black beans, rinsed and drained -2 cans (15 ounces each) – 850 ml
- diced tomatoes, undrained -3 cans (14-1/2 ounces each) -1275 ml
- ground cinnamon -1 tsp. 4 g
- onion, chopped -1 large
- olive oil -2 tbsp.
- pepper - 1/4 tsp. 1 g
- orange juice or juice - 1 cup – 240 ml
- chili powder --1 tsp. 4 g
- garlic cloves, minced -3
- green pepper, -1 medium
- ground cumin-1 tsp. 4 g

Preparation

1. At a moderately high temperature, Oil should be heated in a Dutch oven. The onion and green pepper should be cooked and stirred for 8 to 10 minutes, or until tender. The seasonings should be added after one more minute of boiling.
2. Add the rest of the ingredients and stir as it cooks. Reduce the heat to low, cover the pan, and simmer for 20 to 25 minutes to allow the flavours to mingle.

Nutrition Information

Calories 315, Fat 6.1 g, Total Carbohydrate 52.7g, Total Sugars 8.8g, Protein 15.7g, Potassium 1350 mg, Sodium 15 mg

Storage: a sealed container is used to store Black Bean-Tomato Chili for up to 3 -4 days

Reheat: just defrost at room temperature for a few hours

8.4 Stir-Fry Rice Bowl

Preparation: 15 minutes

Cooking time: 20 minutes

Servings: 4

Ingredients

- bean sprouts -1 cup -180 g
- fresh baby spinach -1 cup 30 g
- canola oil -1 tbsp . 15 ml
- hot cooked brown rice -3 cups – 400 g
- chili garlic sauce -1 tbsp. 15 ml
- sesame oil -1 tsp. 4 ml
- reduced-sodium soy sauce -1 tbsp. 15 ml
- baby portobello mushrooms -1/2 cup sliced – 35 g
- zucchini, -1 medium
- eggs -4 large
- water -1 tbsp. 15 ml
- carrots, -2 medium

Preparation

1. The canola oil needs to be heated over medium-high heat in a big skillet. Add the mushrooms, zucchini, and carrots after they are tender-crisp. For 3 to 5 minutes, simmer while stirring. Water, spicy sauce, spinach, and bean sprouts should all be added. Spinach should only be heated and stirred until it wilts. Stop using the heat and stay cosy.
2. Place 1-2 inches of water in a sizable skillet with high edges. Reduce the heat to a gentle simmer after bringing to a boil. One at a time, crack a cold egg into a tiny bowl and carefully lower it within while keeping the bowl just over the water's surface.
3. Cook, uncovered, for 3 to 5 minutes, or until the yolks are just starting to thicken but are still runny in the centre and the whites are entirely set. The eggs should be taken out of the water with a slotted spoon.
4. When rice is served, vegetables should be put on top of the rice. Add a bit of

sesame oil on top. Put a poached egg on top of each plate.

Nutrition Information

Calories 179, Fat 3.5 g, Total Carbohydrate 24.6g, Total Sugars 4.4g, Protein 10.5g, Potassium 455 mg, Sodium 822 mg

Storage:a sealed container is used to store Stir-Fry Rice Bowl for up to 3 -4 days

Reheat: just defrost at room temperature for a few hours

8.5 Cumin Quinoa Patties

Preparation: 15 minutes

Cooking time: 15 minutes

Servings: 4

Ingredients

- panko bread crumbs -1/4 cup – 27 g
- pepper -1/8 tsp . – pinch
- olive oil -2 tbsp. 30 ml
- green onions, chopped – 3
- large egg, lightly beaten – 1
- Water -1 cup – 240 ml
- salt -1/4 tsp. 1 g
- carrot, cut into 1-inch pieces -1 medium
- cannellini beans, -1 cup – 180 g
- ground cumin -3 tsp. – 12 g
- quinoa, rinsed -1/2 cup – 85 g

Preparation

1. 1. In a small saucepan, heat some water until it boils. is quinoa. Simmer for 12 to 15 minutes, or until all liquid has been absorbed, on low heat with the lid on. Remove the meal from the heat using a fork.
2. In the meantime, the carrot should be processed until it is roughly chopped. To chop the beans, add them and pulse once more. The ingredients should be combined in a big basin. Add the egg, seasonings, bread crumbs, green onions, and cooked quinoa to the mixture. Create 8 patties using the ingredients.

3. The temperature of a large skillet should be set to medium. After placing the patties in the pan, fry them for three to four minutes on each side, or until an instant-read thermometer reads 160° F (71°C). If desired, garnish with salsa, sour cream, and finely chopped fresh cilantro.

Nutrition Information

Calories 352, Fat 10.6 g, Total Carbohydrate 49.3g, Total Sugars 2.6g, Protein 17g, Potassium 906 mg, Sodium 243 mg

Storage:a sealed container is used to store Cumin Quinoa Patties for up to 3 -4 days

Reheat: just defrost at room temperature for a few hours

8.6 Spinach Quesadillas

Preparation: 15 minutes

Cooking time:10 minutes

Servings: 4

Ingredients

- shredded reduced-fat Monterey Jack cheese - 1 cup -28 g
- tomato, chopped -1 small
- ground cumin -1 tsp. 4 g
- fresh baby spinach (about 4 cups) -3 ounces – 85 g
- garlic powder -1/4 tsp. 1 g
- green onions, chopped -4
- Reduced-fat sour cream, optional
- lemon juice -2 tbsp. 30 ml
- 6 flour tortillas (6 inches)
- reduced-fat ricotta cheese -1/4 cup – 30 g

Preparation

1. In a large nonstick skillet, heat the first six ingredients while frequently turning until the spinach has wilted. Once the heat has been turned off, add the cheeses.
2. Before folding over the filling, place one half of each tortilla over the spinach mixture. Cook the meal for 1

to 2 minutes on each side, or until golden brown, on a griddle that has been coated with cooking spray. Quesadillas must be cut in half, and sour cream may be added if preferred.

Nutrition Information

Calories 198, Fat 7.6 g, Total Carbohydrate 21.1g, Total Sugars 1.6g, Protein 13.1g, Potassium 321 mg, Sodium 238 mg

Storage:a sealed container is used to store Spinach Quesadillas for up to 3 -4 days

Reheat: just defrost at room temperature for a few hours

8.7 Ricotta-Stuffed Portobello Mushrooms

Preparation: 15 minutes

Cooking time: 15 minutes

Servings: 6

Ingredients

- minced fresh parsley -2 tbsp. – 6 g
- portobello mushrooms -6 large
- large tomato -6 slices
- pepper -1/8 tsp. 1 g
- reduced-fat ricotta cheese -3/4 cup- 95 g
- water -2 to 3 tsp. 4g
- shredded part-skim mozzarella cheese - 1/2 cup -62 g
- olive oil -2 tbsp. 30 ml
- grated Parmesan cheese, divided -3/4 cup – 95 g
- fresh basil leaves -3/4 cup - 4 g
- slivered almonds or pine nuts, toasted - 3 tbsp. – 45g
- garlic clove -1 small

Preparation

1. 1 tablespoon of ricotta cheese Combine the pepper, parsley, mozzarella cheese, and parmesan cheese in a small bowl. Mushroom stems should be removed and discarded. Use a spoon to scrape the gills out. Fill caps with ricotta

mixture. Slices of tomato may be added.

2. Cover the grill and cook the mushrooms for 8 to 10 minutes over medium heat. When removing something from the grill, use a metal spatula.

3. Basil, almonds, and garlic should all be added to a small food processor and pulsed until minced while waiting. The remaining Parmesan cheese should be added and mixed briefly. Add water and oil in stages as you process to achieve the correct consistency. Before serving, spoon over the stuffed mushrooms.

Nutrition Information

Calories 143, Fat 9.8 g, Total Carbohydrate 6.4g, Total Sugars 0.6g , Protein 9.2g, Potassium 414 mg, Sodium 87 mg

Storage:a sealed container is used to store Ricotta-Stuffed Portobello Mushrooms for up to 3 -4 days

Reheat: just defrost at room temperature for a few hours

8.8 Tomato & Avocado Sandwiches

Preparation: 15 minutes
Cooking time: 10 minutes
Servings: 2
Ingredients

- tomato, sliced -1 medium
- ripe avocado, -1/2 medium
- whole wheat bread, toasted -4 slices
- finely chopped shallot -2 tbsp. 30 g
- hummus -1/4 cup – 62 g

Preparation

1. On top of two slices of toast, spread avocado. Add tomato and shallot on top. The remaining toast slices should be topped with hummus and placed face down on top of the tomato layer of the avocado toast.

Nutrition Information

Calories 311, Fat 14.8 g,Total Carbohydrate 36g, Total Sugars 5g, Protein 11.5g, Potassium 633 mg, Sodium 390 mg

Storage:a sealed container is used to store Tomato & Avocado Sandwiches for up to 3 -4 days

Reheat: just defrost at room temperature for a few hours

8.9 Creamy Fettuccine with Brussels Sprouts & Mushrooms

Preparation: 15 minutes
Cooking time: 15 minutes
Servings: 6
Ingredients

- finely shredded Asiago cheese, plus more for garnish - 1 cup -28 g
- sherry vinegar -2 tbsp. 30 ml
- freshly ground pepper -½ tsp -2 g
- all-purpose flour -2 tbsp. 30 g
- salt -½ tsp. 2 g
- garlic -1 tbsp. – 15 g
- sliced Brussels sprouts -4 cups- 350 g
- extra-virgin olive oil -1 tbsp. – 15 ml
- mixed mushrooms -4 cups – 280 g
- whole-wheat fettuccine -12 ounces
- low-fat milk -2 cups – 480 ml
- finely shredded Asiago cheese, plus more for garnish - 1 cup -28 g

Preparation

1. Cook the pasta for 8 to 10 minutes, or until it's al dente, in a large pot of boiling water. Drain, then add to the pot.

2. While you wait, heat the oil in a big skillet over medium heat. Brussels sprouts and mushrooms should be cooked together for 8 to 10 minutes, stirring often, or until the mushrooms have lost their liquid. The garlic should be stir-fried for about a minute after being added, or until fragrant. Before

adding the sherry, take sure to remove any lingering brown particles (or vinegar). If you're using vinegar, bring it to a boil while stirring, then simmer it for 10 to 30 seconds, or until almost all the liquid has evaporated (if using sherry).

3. Add the milk and flour you've blended in a different bowl to the skillet along with the salt and pepper. Cook the sauce, stirring often, for about 2 minutes, or until it bubbles and thickens. Add the Asiago and whisk until melted. Combine the pasta and sauce in a gentle stir. Add more cheese to the dish's top if you'd like.

Nutrition Information

Calories 312, Fat 5.8 g, Total Carbohydrate 47.3g, Total Sugars 6.3g, Protein 16.7g, Potassium 509 mg, Sodium 314 mg

Storage: a sealed container is used to store Creamy Fettuccine with Brussels Sprouts & Mushrooms for up to 3 -4 days

Reheat: just defrost at room temperature for a few hours

8.10 Pepper Ricotta Primavera

Preparation: 10 minutes
Cooking time: 10 minutes
Servings: 6

Ingredients

- green pepper, -1 medium
- dried basil -1/4 tsp. – 2g
- zucchini, sliced 1 medium
- garlic clove, minced – 1
- frozen peas, thawed -1 cup -80 g
- sweet yellow pepper, julienned-1 medium
- fettuccine, cooked and drained -6 ounces – 760 g
- olive oil -4 tsp. -16 ml
- dried oregano -1/4 tsp. – 2g
- crushed red pepper flakes -1/2 tsp. – 2g
- part-skim ricotta cheese -1 cup -124 g
- sweet red pepper, julienned -1 medium
- milk -1/2 cup -120 ml

Preparation

1. Ricotta cheese and milk are combined, then set aside. Oil should be heated over medium heat in a big skillet. For a minute, add the garlic and pepper flakes. the next seven components. The goal is for vegetables to be crisp-tender, which takes about 5 minutes of cooking and stirring at medium heat.

2. Pasta with a cheese mixture and vegetables on top. Coat by tossing. Serve right away.

Nutrition Information

Calories 219, Fat 7.4 g, Total Carbohydrate 28.2g, Total Sugars 4.5g, Protein 11.1g, Potassium 393 mg, Sodium 94 mg

Storage: a sealed container is used to store Pepper Ricotta Primavera for up to 3 -4 days

Reheat: just defrost at room temperature for a few hours

8.11 Chickpea Curry

Preparation: 10 minutes
Cooking time: 10 minutes
Servings: 6

Ingredients

- fresh ginger, peeled and coarsely chopped -1 2-inch
- canola oil or grapeseed oil -6 tbsp.-90 g
- can diced tomatoes with their juice - 2 ¼ cups
- ground turmeric -½ tsp. 2 g
- kosher salt -¾ tsp – 3 g
- ground cumin -2 tsp . 8 g
- cloves garlic -4 large
- ground coriander -2 tsp- 8 g
- yellow onion, chopped (1-inch) -1 medium
- cans chickpeas, rinsed -2 15-ounce – 850 g
- garam masala -2 tsp.- 8 g
- Fresh cilantro for garnish

Preparation

1. The ginger, garlic, and serrano peppers should all be chopped up very finely before blending. Once you've scraped the sidewalls, recheck your pulse. When the onion is added, pulse several times until it is roughly chopped but not wet.
2. In a sizable saucepan, heat the oil to a medium-high temperature. Add the onion combination and simmer for 3 to 5 minutes, or until softened, while stirring regularly. Continuously whisk in the coriander, cumin, and turmeric.
3. To obtain finely chopped tomatoes, pulse the tomatoes in the food processor. Salt should also be added to the pan. Cook on low heat for four minutes to maintain a simmer., stirring regularly. Garam masala and chickpeas are added, the heat is reduced to a gentle simmer, the pan is covered, and cooking is continued for an additional five minutes with frequent stirring. Add cilantro as a garnish if preferred after serving.

Nutrition Information

Calories 655, Fat 22.8 g, Total Carbohydrate 89.2g, Total Sugars 16g, Protein 27.9g, Potassium 1301 mg, Sodium 323 mg

Storage: a sealed container is used to store Chickpea Curry for up to 3 -4 days

Reheat: just defrost at room temperature for a few hours

8.12 Asparagus Tofu Stir-Fry

Preparation: 15 minutes
Cooking time: 10 minutes
Servings: 4

Ingredients

- pepper -1/4 tsp. -1 g
- asparagus, trimmed and cut into 1-inch pieces -1 pound – 450 g
- vegetable broth - 1-1/4 cups – 300 ml
- extra-firm tofu, drained and cut into 1/2-inch cubes -1 package (14 ounces) -400 g
- reduced-sodium soy sauce -4 tsp – 16 g
- sliced almonds, toasted -2 tbsp. 30 g
- salt -1/4 tsp. -1 g
- canola oil, divided -3 tsp. – 12 g
- minced fresh gingerroot, divided - 2 tsp . 8 g
- Cornstarch -1 tbsp -15 g
- yellow summer squash, halved and sliced -1 medium
- green onions, thinly sliced – 2
- hot cooked brown rice -2 cups -300 g
- Sugar -1/2 tsp . 2 g

Preparation

1. In a small bowl, combine the cornflour, sugar, broth, and soy sauce.
2. In a big non-stick skillet or wok, stir-fry 1 teaspoon ginger in 1 teaspoon oil for 1 minute. It is required to stir the asparagus for two minutes. The squash is added after stirring for a further two minutes. Add the onions after the veggies are crisp-tender and stir-fry for a further minute. Keep hot after removal.
3. The tofu is stir-fried with the remaining ginger, salt, and pepper for 7-9 minutes, or until lightly browned. Keep hot after removal.
4. After stirring, add the cornflour mixture to the pan. Cook and stir for 2 minutes, or until thickened, after coming to a boil. once the tofu and asparagus mixture has fully heated. Before presenting rice with almonds on top, add rice.

Nutrition Information

Calories 227, Fat 7.6 g, Total Carbohyrate 32.8g, Total Sugars 4.2g, Protein 9.7g, Potassium 572 mg, Sodium 525mg

Storage: a sealed container is used to store Asparagus Tofu Stir-Fry for up to 3 -4 days

Reheat: just defrost at room temperature for a few hours

8.13 Mushroom & Tofu Stir-Fry

Preparation: 15 minutes
Cooking time 10 minutes
Servings: 5

Ingredients

- grated fresh ginger 1 tbsp. – 15 g
- clove garlic, grated -1 large
- scallions, trimmed and cut into 2-inch pieces -1 bunch
- peanut oil or canola oil, divided -4 tbsp. – 60 ml
- baked tofu or smoked tofu, diced -1 (8 ounce) container – 230 g
- mixed mushrooms, sliced -1 pound – 450 g
- oyster sauce -3 tbsp.- 45 ml
- red bell pepper, diced -1

Preparation

1. Heat two teaspoons of oil over high heat in a sizable flat-bottomed cast-iron skillet or wok. Simmer the vegetables for 4 minutes, tossing them regularly, until they are soft after adding the bell pepper and mushrooms. Add the scallions, ginger, and garlic after 30 more seconds. Add the vegetables to a bowl.
2. Add the remaining 2 tablespoons of oil to the skillet along with the tofu. Cook until browned for 3 to 4 minutes, turning once. Oyster sauce and vegetables are combined. Cook for approximately a minute, frequently stirring, until heated.

Nutrition Information

Calories 240, Fat 22.2 g, Total Carbohydrate 9.8g, Total Sugars 2g , Protein 7.3g, Potassium 183 mg, Sodium 722 mg
Storage: a sealed container is used to store Mushroom & Tofu Stir-Fry for up to 3 -4 days
Reheat: just defrost at room temperature for a few hours

8.14 Greek Sandwich Bites

Preparation: 15 minutes
Cooking time: 05 minutes
Servings: 16

Ingredients

- crumbled feta cheese -1 cup (4 ounces) – 112 g
- olive oil -1 tbsp. 15ml
- fresh baby spinach -1 pound – 450 g
- pine nuts, toasted - 1/4 cup – 34 g
- salt -1/4 tsp. 1 g
- butter, softened -4 tsp. 32 g
- pepper -1/4 tsp. 1 g
- onion, -1 medium
- garlic cloves, minced – 2
- ground nutmeg - 1/8 tsp.
- Italian bread (1/2 inch thick) - 8

Preparation

1. Until transparent, soften onion in oil in a big non-stick skillet. Cook the garlic for an additional minute after adding it. Until it wilts, spinach is cooked, added, and mixed. Drain. Add the feta, pine nuts, salt, pepper, and nutmeg while stirring.
2. Spread the remaining 4 slices of bread, then top with the final slice. Butter should be spread over the exterior of the sandwiches. Grill uncovered for 3–4 minutes, turning once, or until bread is browned and cheese is melted. Four equal pieces should be cut from each sandwich.

Nutrition Information

Calories 79, Fat 5.6 g , Total Carbohydrate 5g, Total Sugars 0.9g, Protein 3g, Potassium 195 mg, Sodium 198 mg
Storage: a sealed container is used to store Greek Sandwich Bites for up to 3 -4 days
Reheat: just defrost at room temperature for a few hours

8.15 Vegetarian Linguine

Preparation: 15 minutes

Cooking time: 15 minutes

Servings: 6

Ingredients

- tomato, chopped -1 large
- shredded Parmesan cheese - 3 tbsp. – 45 g
- salt - 1/2 tsp. – 2 g
- garlic clove, minced – 1
- uncooked linguine -6 ounces – 770 g
- shredded provolone cheese - 1 cup – 132 g
- pepper - 1/4 tsp. 1 g
- olive oil -1 tbsp. 15 ml
- mushrooms, - 1/2 pound – 250 g
- green onions, chopped – 2
- zucchini, -2 medium
- butter -2 tbsp. – 30 g
- minced fresh basil - 2 tsp. – 8 g

Preparation

1. Prepare the linguine according to the instructions on the package. Meanwhile, heat oil and butter in a large skillet over medium heat. After adding the mushrooms and zucchini, cook them for 3 to 5 minutes. The addition of tomato, onions, garlic, and spices. Reduce the heat, cover the pot, and simmer for about three minutes.
2. Combine the linguine that has been cooked with the veggie mixture. Basil and cheese ought to be added. Throw to coat.

Nutrition Information

Calories 284, Fat 16 g , Total Carbohydrate 21.7g, Total Sugars 2.8g, Protein 15.8g, Potassium 463 mg, Sodium 562 mg

Storage: a sealed container is used to store Vegetarian Linguine for up to 3 -4 days

Reheat: just defrost at room temperature for a few hours

9   VEGAN DISHES

9.1   Tofu Scramble

Preparation: 05 minutes

Cooking time 10 minutes

Servings: 2

Ingredients

- turmeric (optional)- 1/2 tsp.- 2 g
- Fresh lemon juice to garnish
- red onion (chopped) -1/2 medium
- cumin powder-1 tsp. 4 g
- tomato (chopped with seeds removed) -1
- sea salt -1/2 tsp.- 2 g
- Fresh coriander to garnish
- chili powder -1/4 tsp. – 1g
- green bell pepper (chopped with seeds removed) -1
- Oil or butter for coating the pan
- firm tofu (drained) - 16 oz. – 450 g
- garlic powder -1 tsp. 4 g
- water -1 tbsp. 15ml

Preparation

1. Cut the bell pepper, tomato, and onion into cubes.
2. Warm up the pan with some butter or oil. Bell pepper, tomato, and onions should all be added to the pan to soften. for three minutes.
3. Tofu should be crumbled and added to the pan with the vegetables while being stirred.
4. The spices should be mixed together in a small basin. The spices should be combined with 1 tablespoon of water before being added to the tofu scramble and thoroughly stirred.
5. Cook for 5 minutes to let the flavours meld, then serve with a squeeze of fresh lemon, if desired.

Nutrition Information

Calories 211, Fat 10.1 g, Total Carbohydr ate 15.3g , Total Sugars 7.6g, Protein 20.5g, Potassium 688 mg, Sodium 507mg

Storage: Any additional tofu scramble can simply be refrigerated for 3-5 days in an airtight container.

Reheat: just defrost at room temperature for a few hours

9.2 Chickpea & Potato Curry

Preparation: 15 minutes
Cooking time 20 minutes
Servings: 4

Ingredients

- salt -¾ tsp. -3 g
- cayenne pepper -¼ tsp. – 1 g
- low-sodium chickpeas, rinsed -1 (15 ounce) can – 425 g
- onion, diced -1 large
- Yukon Gold potatoes, -1 pound -450 g
- garlic, minced -3 cloves
- Garam masala -½ tsp. – 2 g
- diced tomatoes -1 (14 ounce) can -400 g
- curry powder -2 tsp. – 8g
- water, divided -¾ cup – 180 ml
- grapeseed oil or canola oil -3 tbsp. 45 ml
- frozen peas -1 cup -80 g

Preparation

1. In a big saucepan with a steamer basket attached, bring 1 inch of water to a boil. Potatoes should be steamed for 6 to 8 minutes, covered, or until they are soft. Separate the potatoes. As the pot dries

2. In a pot, heat the oil to a medium-high temperature. When the onion is done, add it and cook it, stirring regularly for 3 to 5 minutes, until it is transparent. Stirring often, saute the garlic, curry powder, salt, and cayenne for one minute. Cook for two minutes after adding the tomatoes and their juice. Fill

a blender or food processor with the ingredients. Using 1/2 cup of water, blend until completely smooth.

3. Add more purée to the pot. To remove any excess sauce, blend or process the remaining 1/4 cup water. Potatoes, peas, and chickpeas that were set aside should be combined with the garam masala in the pot. About five minutes of continual stirring while heating.

Nutrition Information

Calories 585, Fat 17g , Total Carbohydrate 87g, Total Sugars 18.2g, Protein 24.9g, Potassium 1237 mg, Sodium 512 mg

Storage:curry can simply be refrigerated for 3-5 days in an airtight container.

Reheat: just defrost at room temperature for a few hours

9.3 Cauliflower Alfredo Sauce

Preparation: 10 minutes
Cooking time 05 minutes
Servings: 4

Ingredients

- Pepper to taste (I used 1 tsp.)
- onion (diced) -1 medium
- freshly squeezed lemon juice -1 tsp. – 4 g
- vegetable broth -1 cup – 240 ml
- sea salt -1/2 tsp. – 2 g
- chopped cauliflower florets -4 cups – 400 g
- olive oil -1 tbsp. 15 ml
- chili flakes (optional) -1 tsp. 4 g
- nutritional yeast -1 tbsp. 15g
- Vegan butter -2 tbsp. 30 g
- garlic cloves – 2

Preparation

1. In a pot on medium-high heat, warm the oil. Add the onion to the hot oil once it is hot, and cook it for three to five minutes, or until it is translucent and soft.

2. Cook the garlic for 30 seconds after adding it.
3. Cauliflower florets and vegetable stock should be added to the saucepan before it is tightly covered. Cauliflower should be tender after 5 minutes of steaming.
4. Blend the soft cauliflower until it is smooth and creamy in your blender on high. If the cauliflower is difficult to combine, add one tablespoon of broth at a time.
5. Blend the steamed cauliflower in a blender with the vegan butter, nutritional yeast, salt, pepper, lemon juice, and chilli flakes.
6. When the sauce has the consistency you want, blend all the components together.
7. Serve immediately with low-carb spaghetti or vegetarian noodles.

Nutrition Information
Calories 138, Fat 9.9 g, Total Carbohydrate 9.8g, Total Sugars 3.8g, Protein 4.8g, Potassium 465 mg, Sodium 499 mg
Storage:a sealed container is used to store Cauliflower Alfredo Sauce for up to 3 -4 days
Reheat: just defrost at room temperature for a few hours

9.4 Cauliflower Pizza with Basil Pesto

Preparation: 20 minutes
Cooking time 1 hr.10 minutes
Servings: 4
Ingredients
For the cauliflower pizza base:
- almond flour -1/3 cup – 14 g
- cauliflower rice -4 cups – 400g
- dried oregano -2 tsp. -8g
- onion powder -1/2 tsp. – 2 g
- water -5 tbsp.-75 ml
- flax seed meal -2 tbsp. – 30 g
- sea salt -1/2 tsp. – 2 g
- 4 basil leaves (chopped)

For the basil pesto:
- pine nuts -3 tablespoons – 24 g
- fresh basil leaves -2 cups –
- sea salt and black pepper to taste
- olive oil -3 tbsp. – 45 ml
- lemon juice -1 tablespoon – 15 ml
- nutritional yeast -2 tablespoon – 30 g
- 2 cloves garlic

Preparation
1. Set your oven's temperature to 375 degrees Fahrenheit (190 C).
2. Cut a big head of cauliflower into smaller florets to make homemade cauliflower rice. Use a box grater with medium-sized holes or the grater attachment on your food processor to shred these florets. alternative: riced cauliflower is an option.
3. The riced cauliflower is put into a big saucepan of boiling water. After combining and boiling for 5 minutes, the rice ought to be tender.
4. Drain the cauliflower rice using a dishtowel or a colander with a fine mesh. After the majority of the water has been drained, let the rice aside for 5 minutes to cool.
5. While the cauliflower rice cools, combine the flaxseed meal and water, form a ball, and set it aside. Set aside.
6. After the cauliflower rice has cooled, press out as much water as you can by wrapping it in a dish towel. As much moisture as you can must be removed.
7. Combine the cooked cauliflower rice, ground flaxseed, almond flour, oregano, onion powder, sea salt, and finely chopped basil leaves in a big mixing dish.
8. Use your hands to thoroughly mix the items.
9. Spread the dough and make a circle with it on a baking sheet that has been dusted with gluten-free flour. It should be roughly half an inch (1.5 cm) thick overall, with somewhat thicker edges.

10. After 30 minutes, take the crust out of the oven.

11. Add your preferred garnishes and a thin coating of tomato sauce after that. Bake for a further 10 to 15 minutes, or until the base is cooked through and the sides are golden brown.

12. Combine all the ingredients for the basil pesto in a food processor and process until smooth while the pizza bakes. Add more water if the mixture isn't combining well.

13. After being taken out of the oven and topped with freshly made basil pesto, pizza should be served hot.

Nutrition Information

Calories 288, Fat 22.2 g, Total Carbohydrate 14.1g, Total Sugars 4.5g, Protein 10g, Potassium 215 mg, Sodium 363 mg

Storage: a sealed container is used to store Cauliflower Pizza with Basil Pesto for up to 3 - 4 days

Reheat: just defrost at room temperature for a few hours

9.5 Squash with Garlic & Parsley

Preparation: 15 minutes
Cooking time 10 minutes
Servings: 10

Ingredients

- Garlic -3 cloves
- winter squash , -5 pounds – 2.2 Kg
- Italian parsley -2 tbsp. – 8 g
- extra-virgin olive oil, divided -2 tbsp. - 30 ml
- freshly ground pepper, divided -¼ tsp.- 1g
- salt -1 ½ tsp. – 6g

Preparation

1. Set the oven to 375 degrees Fahrenheit (190 C).

2. Combine the squash with 1/4 teaspoon each of salt, pepper, and 4 teaspoons of oil. Spread it evenly across a sizable

baking sheet. Roast for 30 to 45 minutes, tossing regularly, or until softly browned and uniformly cooked (depending on the variety of squash).

3. In a little saucepan set over medium heat, warm the 2 tablespoons of remaining oil. Stirring regularly, add the garlic and simmer for 30 to 60 seconds, or until fragrant but not browned. Combine the parsley, garlic, and roasted butternut squash. following flavouring, serving, and tasting.

Nutrition Information

Calories 116, Fat 3 g, Total Carbohydrate 24g, Total Sugars 0g, Protein 1.9g, Potassium 795 mg, Sodium 7 mg

Storage: a sealed container is used to store Squash with Garlic & Parsley for up to 3 -4 days

Reheat: just defrost at room temperature for a few hours

9.6 Stuffed Potatoes with Salsa & Beans

Preparation: 15 minutes
Cooking time 10 minutes
Servings: 4

Ingredients

- fresh salsa -½ cup –65 g
- avocado, sliced -1 ripe
- pinto beans, rinsed, warmed and lightly mashed -1 (15 ounce) can – 450 g
- russet potatoes -4 medium
- chopped pickled jalapeños -4 tsp.- 16 g

Preparation

1. Use a fork to pierce potatoes all over. For around 20 minutes, on Medium, flip the food once or twice until soft. (Alternatively, bake potatoes for 45 to 1 hour at 425 degrees F until they are soft.) After transferring, allow it cool somewhat on a clean cutting board.

2. 2. Holding the potato with a dish towel to protect your hands, make a longitudinal cut, but don't go all the

way through. Pinch the ends to uncover the flesh.

3. Add some salsa, avocado, beans, and jalapenos on the top of each potato. Serve hot

Nutrition Information

Calories 632, Fat 11.8 g, Total Carbohydrate 106.8g , Total Sugars 5.9g, Protein 27.3g, Potassium 183 mg, Sodium 722 mg

Storage: a sealed container is used to store Stuffed Potatoes with Salsa & Beans for up to 3 -4 days

Reheat: just defrost at room temperature for a few hours

9.7 Butternut Squash & Root Vegetables

Preparation: 10 minutes
Cooking time 30 minutes
Servings: 4

Ingredients

- sliced parsnips -1 cup – 133 g
- ground pepper -⅛ tsp.
- cayenne pepper -⅛ tsp.
- chopped onion -½ cup – 58 g
- olive oil -1 tbsp. 15 ml
- butternut squash, -3 cups
- salt -¼ tsp. 1g
- sliced carrot -½ cup – 64 g

Preparation

1. Set the oven's temperature to 400°F (204°C). A baking dish that is 15 by 10 inches should be filled with squash, parsnips, carrots, and onions.
2. Season the vegetables with salt, pepper, and cayenne, then toss to cover with oil.
3. Roast covered for 20 minutes. After giving the vegetables a stir, roast them uncovered for a further 10 minutes, or until they are tender-crisp and starting to colour.

Nutrition Information

Calories 144, Fat 3.7 g, Total Carbohydrate 20.8g, Total Sugars 5.2g, Protein 1.7g, Potassium 559 mg, Sodium 165 mg

Storage: a sealed container is used to store Butternut Squash & Root Vegetables for up to 3 -4 days

Reheat: just defrost at room temperature for a few hours

9.8 Zucchini & Mushroom Sauté

Preparation: 15 minutes
Cooking time 15 minutes
Servings: 4

Ingredients

- Salt & freshly ground pepper, to taste
- extra-virgin olive oil -2 tsp. – 8 ml
- zucchini, julienned -2 small
- chopped fresh basil -2 tsp. – 8 g
- sliced mushrooms -1 ½ cups -105 g

Preparation

1. Use a big non-stick skillet set on high heat to warm the oil. For two minutes, keep stirring after adding the zucchini. While stirring occasionally, the basil and mushrooms should cook for approximately a minute, or until they are tender. Add salt and pepper to taste.

Nutrition Information

Calories 35, Fat 2.2 g, Total Carbohydrate 2.9g, Total Sugars 1.5g, Protein 1.5g, Potassium 239 mg, Sodium 7 mg

Storage: a sealed container is used to store Zucchini & Mushroom Sauté for up to 3 -4 days

Reheat: just defrost at room temperature for a few hours

9.9 Garlicky Green Beans

Preparation: 15 minutes
Cooking time 10 minutes
Servings: 8

Ingredients

- salt -½ tsp. – 2 g

- minced garlic-3 tbsp. – 45 g
- Freshly ground pepper, to taste
- chopped fresh tarragon, 1 tbsp. – 3g
- green beans, trimmed -2 pounds
- extra-virgin olive oil -3 tbsp. – 45 ml
- minced fresh parsley 3 tbsp. – 10 g

Preparation

1. The first step is to heat the water in a large saucepan. Put a sizable bowl of ice water close to the burner.
2. Add half of the green beans to the boiling water and simmer for 4 minutes, or until crisp-tender. With a slotted spoon, add the beans to the cold water to chill. Continue with the remaining beans. Using a slotted spoon, remove the beans from the ice water, and then place them on a baking sheet that has been lined with a kitchen towel. Use a different towel to pat them dry after that.
3. Just before serving, heat oil in a big skillet or Dutch oven over medium heat. After continuously swirling for around 30 seconds, the garlic should start to smell delicious. Green beans may be added; stir. Add the parsley, tarragon, salt, and pepper, and stir-fry for 1 to 3 minutes or until cooked through.

Nutrition Information

Calories 85, Fat 5.4 g, Total Carbohydrate 9.2g, Total Sugars 1.6g, Protein 2.3g, Potassium 258 mg, Sodium 155 mg

Storage: a sealed container is used to store Garlicky Green Beans for up to 3 -4 days

Reheat: just defrost at room temperature for a few hours

9.10 Broccoli and Cauliflower Sauté

Preparation: 15 minutes
Cooking time 10 minutes
Servings: 4

Ingredients

- Reduced-sodium chicken broth -¼ cup – 60 ml
- olive oil -2 tsp. -8 g
- cauliflower florets -1 cup – 100 g
- garlic, -1 clove
- ground black pepper -⅛ tsp.
- broccoli florets -1 cup – 90 g
- Water -3 tbsp. 45 ml
- Salt -⅛ tsp.

Preparation

1. Bring the oil to a medium-high simmer in a big skillet. The broccoli, cauliflower, and garlic are stir-fried for two minutes. With caution, turn down the heat after adding the wine, water, salt, and pepper. Cook for two minutes while covered.
2. Take off the lid, then control the heat. Vegetables should be sautéed for two minutes or until soft.

Nutrition Information

Calories 47, Fat 2.2 g, Total Carbohydrate 3.5g, Total Sugars 1.1g, Protein 1.2g, Potassium 165 mg, Sodium 16 mg

Storage: a sealed container is used to store Broccoli and Cauliflower Sauté for up to 3 -4 days

Reheat: just defrost at room temperature for a few hours

10 FISH AND SHELLFISH

10.1 Baked Garlicky Salmon Balls

Preparation: 10 minutes

Cooking time 20 minutes

Servings: 4

Ingredients

- Italian breadcrumbs -3 tbsp. -45 g
- Cooking spray
- egg, lightly beaten -1 large
- Scallion, thinly sliced - 1
- minced garlic -1 tbsp. – 15 g
- boneless, skinless salmon, drained -2(6 ounce) cans – 340 g
- low-fat plain strained yogurt -1 tbsp. 15 g

Preparation

1. setting the oven to 400°F (204°C). You can use parchment paper to line a sizable baking sheet with a rim.
2. Combine the salmon, breadcrumbs, scallion, egg, yoghurt, and garlic in a large bowl. Break up the fish as you mix everything together thoroughly. Form a ball out of the dough using clean hands, and place it on the prepared baking sheet. 18 to 20 salmon balls can be made using the remaining ingredients and the same method. Spray the balls with cooking spray sparingly. Bake for about 20 minutes, flipping once, until firm and brown.

Nutrition Information

Calories 158, Fat 6.9 g, Total Carbohydrate 5.1g, Total Sugars 0.8g, Protein 19.2g, Potassium 372 mg, Sodium 95 mg

Storage:a sealed container is used to store Baked Garlicky Salmon Balls for up to 3 -4 days

Reheat: just defrost at room temperature for a few hours

10.2 Red Pepper & Parmesan Tilapia

Preparation: 15 minutes

Cooking time 10 minutes

Servings: 4

Ingredients

- grated Parmesan cheese -1/2 cup -14 g
- tilapia fillets -4 – 680 g
- pepper -1/2 tsp. – 2 g
- egg, lightly beaten -1 large
- crushed red pepper flakes -1/2 to 1 tsp. – 4 g
- Italian seasoning -1 tsp. 4 g

Preparation

1. Oven temperature adjustment to 425 degrees (218 C). In a small bowl, place the egg. Mix the cheese, Italian seasoning, pepper, and red pepper flakes in a separate shallow bowl. After being dipped in egg, fish fillets are then topped in a cheese concoction.
2. Put the fillets in a baking dish that is 15x10x1 inches and has been coated with cooking spray. Bake fish for 10 to 15 minutes, or until it just starts to flake when tested with a fork.

Nutrition Information

Calories 127, Fat 3.4 g, Total Carbohydrate 0.7g, Total Sugars 0.2g   ,   Protein   23.8g, Potassium 25 mg, Sodium 91 mg

Storage:a sealed container is used to store Red Pepper & Parmesan Tilapia for up to 3 -4 days

Reheat: just defrost at room temperature for a few hours

10.3 Garlicky Shrimp & Broccoli

Preparation: 15 minutes

Cooking time 10 minutes

Servings: 4

Ingredients

- cloves garlic, sliced, divided -6 medium
- peeled and deveined raw shrimp -1 pound -450 g
- small broccoli florets -4 cups – 360 g
- ground pepper, divided-½ tsp. – 2g
- diced red bell pepper -½ cup
- lemon juice -2 tsp. – 8 ml
- salt, divided -½ tsp. – 2g
- extra-virgin olive oil, divided -3 tbsp. -45 ml

Preparation

1. A sizable pot with 2 tablespoons of oil over medium heat. For approximately a minute, saute the other half of the garlic until it starts to turn brown. There are also 1/4 teaspoons of salt and pepper, along with broccoli and bell pepper. Add 1 tablespoon of water to the saucepan if it's too dry, then boil it for an additional 3 to 5 minutes with the cover on while stirring once or twice. Warm up in a bowl after transfer.

2. Increase the heat to medium-high and add the final tablespoon of oil. A minute or so later, add the remaining garlic and saute it until it starts to brown. The mixture is boiled for 3 to 5 minutes while being stirred, or until the shrimp are just barely cooked through. Shrimp are then added, along with the remaining 1/4 teaspoon of salt and pepper. Combine the broccoli mixture once more in the pot with the lemon juice.

Nutrition Information

Calories 222, Fat 11.8 g, Total Carbohydrte 6.6g, Total Sugars 0.9g, Protein 25.5g, Potassium 283 mg, Sodium 441 mg

Storage: a sealed container is used to store Garlicky Shrimp & Broccoli for up to 3 -4 days

Reheat: just defrost at room temperature for a few hours

10.4 Salmon with Horseradish Pistachio Crust

Preparation: 15 minutes

Cooking time 15 minutes

Servings: 6

Ingredients

- dry bread crumbs -2/3 cup – 40 g
- shallots -1/2 cup- 80 g
- salmon fillets -6
- olive oil -2 tbsp. – 30 ml
- grated lemon or orange zest -1/2 tsp. – 2 g
- pistachios -2/3 cup – 66 g
- snipped fresh dill -1 tbsp. – 3 g
- crushed red pepper flakes -1/4 tsp. – 1g
- garlic clove -1
- sour cream -1/3 cup – 80 g
- prepared horseradish -1tbsp. – 15 g

Preparation

1. beginning to turn on the oven to 350 degrees (176 C). Place the salmon skin-side down in a 15x10x1-inch baking pan that has not been oiled. Sour cream should be spread over each fillet. combine the remaining ingredients. The crumb-nut mixture should be spread over the tops of the salmon fillets and pushed down to help it adhere. Fish should be baked for 12 to 15 minutes, or until it just begins to flake easily when tested with a fork.

Nutrition Information

Calories 398, Fat 22.2 g, Total Carbohydrate 13.5g, Total Sugars 1.4g, Protein 38.3g, Potassium 849 mg, Sodium 218 mg

Storage: a sealed container is used to store Salmon with Horseradish Pistachio Crust for up to 3 -4 days

Reheat: just defrost at room temperature for a few hours

10.5 Shrimp and Cauliflower Bake

Preparation: 15 minutes

Cooking time 45 minutes

Servings: 4

Ingredients

- salt -¼ tsp. – 1 g
- small cauliflower florets (1 medium head) -4 cups – 400 g
- Lemon wedges – 4
- olive oil -2 tbsp.- 30 ml
- garlic, minced -2 cloves
- crushed red pepper -½ tsp. -2 g
- shrimp -1 pound -450 g
- diced tomatoes, drained -2 (14.5 ounce) cans – 700 g
- chopped onion -½ cup
- snipped fresh dill -1 tbsp. – 15 g
- lemon zest -1 tsp.- 4 g
- crumbled reduced-fat feta cheese -½ cup – 17 g

Preparation

1. Set the oven temperature to 425 degrees (218 C). a sizable bowl, mix the cauliflower, onion, oil, salt, and crushed red pepper. The ingredients should be distributed in a little, shallow metal roasting pan. The cauliflower should only be tender after 25 minutes of baking.
2. Meanwhile, rinse and pat dry the shrimp. Mix the shrimp, tomatoes, garlic, and lemon zest in a medium bowl. On top of the cauliflower mixture, pour the shrimp mixture. Bake the shrimp for a further 15 minutes, or until opaque.
3. Top the shrimp mixture with the cheese and dill mixture. Add lemon slices as a garnish if preferred.

Nutrition Information

Calories 47, Fat 2.2 g, Total Carbohydrate 3.5g, Total Sugars 1.1 g, Protein 1.2g, Potassium 165 mg, Sodium 16 mg

Storage: a sealed container is used to store Shrimp and Cauliflower Bake for up to 3 -4 days

Reheat: just defrost at room temperature for a few hours

10.6 Walnut-Rosemary Crusted Salmon

Preparation: 10 minutes

Cooking time 10 minutes

Servings: 4

Ingredients

- kosher salt -½ tsp. – 2g
- lemon zest -¼ tsp. – 1 g
- honey -½ tsp. – 2g
- garlic, minced -1 clove
- lemon juice -1 tsp. 1g
- Olive oil cooking spray
- panko breadcrumbs -3 tbsp. -45 g
- extra-virgin olive oil -1 tsp.- 4 g
- Dijon mustard -2 tsp.- 8 g
- skinless salmon fillet, fresh or frozen -1 (1 pound) – 450 g
- parsley and lemon wedges for garnish
- fresh rosemary -1 tsp. – 1g
- crushed red pepper -¼ tsp.- 1 g
- walnuts -3 tbsp. -45 g

Preparation

1. Set the oven's temperature to 425 F. (218 C). You can use parchment paper to line a sizable baking sheet with a rim.
2. In a separate bowl, mix the honey, salt, red pepper flakes, rosemary, mustard, garlic, lemon zest, and lemon juice. In a separate little bowl, combine the panko, walnuts, and oil.
3. Set the prepared baking sheet with the fish on it. After coating the fish with the mustard mixture, sprinkle the panko mixture over it and press firmly to help it stick. Apply some frying spray.
4. Depending on thickness, bake the fish for 8 to 12 minutes, or until it flakes easily when tested with a fork.

5. Garnish with parsley, if desired, and serve with lemon wedges.

Nutrition Information

Calories 356, Fat 10.3 g, Total Carbohydrate 11.4g , Total Sugars 0.8g, Protein 18.2g, Potassium 36 mg, Sodium 455 mg

Storage: a sealed container is used to store Walnut-Rosemary Crusted Salmon for up to 3 - 4 days

Reheat: just defrost at room temperature for a few hours

10.7 Tomato Walnut Tilapia

Preparation: 15 minutes
Cooking time 10 minutes
Servings: 4

Ingredients

topping:

- pepper -1/4 tsp. 1 g
- chopped walnuts -1/4 cup – 7 g
- butter -1 tbsp.- 15 g
- tomato, thinly sliced -1 medium
- soft bread crumbs -1/2 cup – 23 g
- Salt -1/4 tsp. 1 g
- 4 tilapia fillets (4 ounces each)-450 g

Preparation

1. Sprinkle salt and pepper over the fillets. When medium-high heat is attained, butter-coated fillets should be fried for two to three minutes on each side.
2. Place the tomato next to the fish on a broiler plate or baking sheet.
3. Spoon the tomato slices on top after combining the topping's ingredients.
4. Broil the dish for 1-2 minutes at a distance of 3 to 4 inches from the fire, or until the topping is lightly browned and the fish just starts to flake easily when tested with a fork.

Nutrition Information

Calories 184, Fat 8.7 g, Total Carbohydrate 4.3g, Total Sugars 1.1g, Protein 23.5g, Potassium 121 mg, Sodium 239 mg

Storage: a sealed container is used to store Tomato Walnut Tilapia for up to 3 -4 days

Reheat: just defrost at room temperature for a few hours

10.8 Creamy Shrimp & Mushroom Pasta

Preparation: 15 minutes
Cooking time 10 minutes
Servings: 4

Ingredients

- fresh button mushrooms - 1 cup – 70 g
- cashews -½ cup – 68 g
- crushed red pepper -½ tsp.- 2g
- finely chopped fresh rosemary -½ tsp.- 2g
- whole milk -½ cup – 120 ml
- whole-wheat linguine -8 ounces -226 g
- grated Parmesan cheese -3 tbsp.-45 g
- reduced-sodium soy sauce -1 tbsp.-15 ml
- extra-virgin olive oil -1 tbsp.-15 ml
- vegetable broth -1 cup – 240 ml
- large raw shrimp (21 to 25 count), -1 pound – 450 g
- garlic, minced -3 cloves

Preparation

1. Bring a significant amount of water to a rapid boil. Prepare the linguine with the sauce as directed on the package. Drain, then set apart.
2. In the meantime, blend the broth and cashews in a food processor. Blend until smooth, about 15 to 20 seconds. Pour into a small bowl after passing through a fine-mesh filter (discard any solids).
3. Bring the oil to a boil in a big, high-sided skillet. Add the mushrooms, garlic, and rosemary once the mushrooms are soft and the garlic is aromatic. Simmer for two to three minutes while stirring often. Add the milk, soy sauce, and cashew mixture. Over medium heat, bring to a boil.

Then, lower the heat to medium-low and simmer, stirring frequently, for 4 to 5 minutes, or until the sauce has thickened. When the shrimp are fully cooked, add them and simmer them for 4 to 5 minutes, stirring regularly. Once the pasta is added, cook it while constantly tossing it in the sauce for about a minute, or until it is thoroughly covered. On top, sprinkle some Parmesan and red pepper flakes.

Nutrition Information

Calories 507, Fat 20.2 g, Total Carbohydrate 39.5g, Total Sugars 3.7g, Protein 42.9g, Potassium 477 mg, Sodium 933 mg

Storage: a sealed container is used to store Creamy Shrimp & Mushroom Pasta for up to 3 -4 days

Reheat: just defrost at room temperature for a few hours

10.9 Broccoli Tuna Casserole

Preparation: 15 minutes

Cooking time 60 minutes

Servings: 8

Ingredients

- shredded Monterey Jack cheese, divided -1 cup – 113 g
- pepper -1/2 tsp. -2 g
- butter, melted -1 tbsp. – 15 g
- corn-starch -1/4 cup
- butter -1 tsp. -4 g
- fat-free milk -2 cups – 480 ml
- onion -1/4 cup
- reduced-sodium chicken broth -1 cup – 240 ml
- panko bread crumbs -1/3 cup – 36 g
- dried thyme-1 tsp.-4 g
- salt -3/4 tsp. – 3 g
- broccoli florets, thawed -4 cups frozen – 400 g
- uncooked whole wheat egg noodles -5 cups
- dried basil -1 tsp.-4 g

- albacore white tuna in water -2 pouches (6.4 ounces each) – 370 g

Preparation

1. turning on the oven to 350 degrees (176 C). The packaging instructions should be followed for cooking and draining noodles. Transfer to a shallow baking dish that is 13x9 inches or 3 quarts in size and has been coated with cooking spray.
2. In the meantime, melt the butter in a sizable nonstick skillet over medium-high heat. Add the onion and stir until it is soft. Before being stirred into the pan, the cornflour, milk, and seasonings are blended in a small bowl. the broth into the mixture. Bring to a boil, then simmer, stirring frequently, for two minutes to thicken. Add the remaining 3/4 cup of melted cheese after bringing the broccoli and tuna to a boil.
3. Completely mix, then serve with noodles. Sprinkle the remaining cheese over top. The dish needs butter that has been melted and bread crumbs. 45 minutes of covered baking. Bake the dish uncovered for a further 15-20 minutes, or until the cheese has melted.

Nutrition Information

Calories 263, Fat 6.7g, Total Carbohydrate 33g, Total Sugars 4g, Protein 17.2g, Potassium 206 mg, Sodium 570 mg

Storage: a sealed container is used to store Broccoli Tuna Casserole for up to 3 -4 days

Reheat: just defrost at room temperature for a few hours

10.10 Salmon with Sun-Dried Tomato Cream Sauce

Preparation: 15 minutes

Cooking time 20 minutes

Servings: 4

Ingredients

- ground pepper, divided -½ tsp.- 2 g
- cooked brown rice - 2 cups -380 g

- Salmon -1 ¼ pounds – 680 g
- dry white wine -⅓ cup – 34 g
- salt, divided -½ tsp.- 2 g
- low-sodium vegetable broth -⅓ cup – 80 ml
- finely chopped shallots -½ cup – 30 g
- chopped fresh parsley -2 tbsp.- 10 g
- heavy cream -⅓ cup – 40 g
- slivered oil-packed sun-dried tomatoes- ½ cup – 30 g

Preparation

1. Place rack in oven's upper third. Turn the broiler on high. A baking sheet should be foil-lined.
2. On the preheated baking pan, arrange the salmon skin-side down. Add one-fourth teaspoons of salt and pepper each. To ensure even browning, broil the pan for 8 to 12 minutes, flipping it once from front to back. Four parts should be cut.
3. Set a large skillet with sun-dried tomato oil to medium heat in the interim. Stir-fry the shallots and sun-dried tomatoes for a minute after adding them. After turning up the heat, add the wine and broth. Cook for approximately 2 minutes, or until the majority of the liquid has evaporated. Reduce heat to medium, stir in cream, and season to taste with the final 1/4 teaspoon each of salt and pepper. Simmer for two minutes. The salmon should be served with the sauce and parsley on top and the rice should be placed on the side.

Nutrition Information
Calories 751, Fat 22.2 g, Total Carbohydrate 78.9g, Total Sugars 1.2g, Protein 52.4g, Potassium 1465 mg, Sodium 589 mg
Storage: a sealed container is used to store Salmon with Sun-Dried Tomato Cream Sauce for up to 3 -4 days
Reheat: just defrost at room temperature for a few hours

10.11 Seasoned Cod

Preparation: 10 minutes
Cooking time 10 minutes
Servings: 8
Ingredients

- Lemon wedges and/or fresh parsley sprigs -8 wedges
- fresh or frozen skinless cod fillets, 3/4- to 1-inch thick -2 pounds – 907 g
- seasoned salt -½ teaspoon – 2 g
- paprika -1 tsp.-4 g

Preparation

1. Heat the broiler. If frozen, defrost the fish. After cleaning, dry the fish using paper towels. Paprika and seasoning salt should be combined in a small basin. Each fish fillet should have the paprika mixture applied on both sides. Fish thickness is measured.
2. Place the fish on the rack of a broiler pan that has been oiled but not heated. Fork-tested fish should flake easily after cooking for 4 to 6 minutes per 1/2 inch of thickness. , which should be grilled four inches away from the flame. If desired, the dish might be garnished with lemon slices or parsley sprigs. nourishes eight.

Nutrition Information
Calories 751, Fat 22.2 g, Total Carbohydrate 78.5g, Total Sugars 1.2g, Protein 52.4g, Potassium 1430 mg, Sodium 589mg
Storage: a sealed container is used to store Seasoned Cod for up to 3 -4 days
Reheat: just defrost at room temperature for a few hours

10.12 Crumb-Coated Red Snapper

Preparation: 15 minutes
Cooking time 10 minutes
Servings: 4
Ingredients

- salt -1/4 tsp. 1 g

- Red snapper fillets (6 ounces each) – 4 – 680 g
- olive oil -2 tbsp. -30 ml
- lemon-pepper seasoning -1 tsp.-4 g
- grated Parmesan cheese -2 tbsp.-30 g
- dry bread crumbs -1/2 cup -54 g

Preparation

1. Combine the bread crumbs, cheese, salt, pepper, and lemon juice in a small bowl. Add the fillets one at a time and turn to coat.
2. In a large skillet with oil over medium heat, cook fish fillets in batches until the fish just starts to flake easily with a fork, about 4-5 minutes on each side..

Nutrition Information

Calories 377, Fat 13.7 g, Total Carbohydrate 10.6g, Total Sugars 0.8g, Protein 51.2g, Potassium 921 mg, Sodium 473 mg

Storage:a sealed container is used to store Crumb-Coated Red Snapper for up to 3 -4 days

Reheat: just defrost at room temperature for a few hours

10.13 Lemony Parsley Baked Cod

Preparation: 15 minutes

Cooking time 10 minutes

Servings: 4

Ingredients

- grated lemon zest -1 tbsp. – 15 g
- lemon juice -2 tbsp. – 30 ml
- pepper -1/8 tsp.
- garlic cloves, minced -2
- green onions, chopped -2
- olive oil -1 tbsp.-15 ml
- salt -1/4 tsp. -1 g
- minced fresh parsley -3 tbsp.- 12 g
- cod fillets 4 – 680 g

Preparation

1. Warm the oven to 400° (204°C). In a small bowl, combine the first seven ingredients. An 11x7-inch baking dish

that has not been greased should be used to bake the cod. On top, sprinkle some green onions. Bake the fish for 10-15 minutes under cover, or until it flakes easily.

Nutrition Information

Calories 129, Fat 4.6 g, Total Carbohydrate 1.8g, Total Sugars 0.5g , Protein 20.4g, Potassium 57 mg, Sodium 222 mg

Storage:a sealed container is used to store Lemony Parsley Baked Cod for up to 3 -4 days

Reheat: just defrost at room temperature for a few hours

10.14 Lemony Grilled Salmon Fillets with Dill Sauce

Preparation: 15 minutes

Cooking time 10 minutes

Servings: 4

Ingredients

- 2 medium lemons
- 4 salmon fillets (6 ounces each) -680 g

lemon-dill sauce:

- lemon slices, quartered - 3
- dried chervil -1/8 teaspoon
- lemon juice -1/3 cup
- corn-starch -2-1/2 tsp.- 10 g
- Dash cayenne pepper
- salt -1/4 teaspoon – 1g
- snipped fresh dill -1 tbsp.-4 g
- butter -4 tsp.- 16 g
- water -1/2 cup – 120 ml

Preparation

1. Trim the ends of each lemon before cutting it into thick sections. Grill the salmon and lemon slices covered over high heat on an oiled grill rack for 3 to 5 minutes on each side, or until the fish flakes easily with a fork and the slices are lightly browned. You can also broil the food 3 to 4 inches away from the heat for the same amount of time.

2. To make the sauce, mix the cornflour, water, and lemon juice in a small pot. Over medium heat, cook while stirring until the liquid bubbles and thickens. Add the seasonings and the quartered lemon segments after taking the skillet off the heat. Serve with lemon slices and grilled fish.

Nutrition Information

Calories 290, Fat 15.1 g, Total Carbohydrate 4.8g, Total Sugars 1.2g, Protein 35.2g, Potassium 778 mg, Sodium 260 mg

Storage: a sealed container is used to store Lemony Grilled Salmon Fillets with Dill Sauce for up to 3 -4 days

Reheat: just defrost at room temperature for a few hours

11 SIDES AND SMALL PLATES

11.1 Roasted Honeynut Squash

Preparation: 10 minutes
Cooking time 30 minutes
Servings: 4

Ingredients

- salt -¼ tsp. – 1 g
- honeynut squash -2 medium
- ground pepper -¼ tsp. – 1 g
- pure maple syrup (Optional) -4 tsp. – 16ml
- ground cinnamon -¼ tsp. – 1 g
- butter -4 tsp. -16 g

Preparation

1. Set oven to 425 degrees Fahrenheit (218 C).
2. On a baking sheet, squash halves should be arranged cut-side up. With one tablespoon, butter each cavity. Add some cinnamon, pepper, and salt. Roast until soft, about 25 to 30 minutes. If you'd like, drizzle with maple syrup.

Nutrition Information

Calories 67, Fat 4 g, Total Carbohydrate 7.8g, Total Sugars 5.7g, Protein 1.4g, Potassium 274 mg, Sodium 185 mg

Storage: a sealed container is used to store Roasted Honeynut Squash for up to 3 -4 days

Reheat: just defrost at room temperature for a few hours

11.2 Garlic Asiago Cauliflower Rice

Preparation: 10 minutes
Cooking time 10 minutes
Servings: 6

Ingredients

- extra virgin olive oil -1 tbsp. – 15 ml
- head cauliflower -1 medium – 575 g
- garlic-herb seasoning blend -1-1/2 tsp. – 6 g
- Asiago cheese -1/2 cup – 17 g
- unsalted butter -2 tbsp.-30 g

Preparation

1. To finely shred the cauliflower, use a box grater or a food processor with a steel blade (about 6 cups).
2. Melt the butter, oil, and spice mixture over medium-high heat in a large cast-iron skillet or other substantial skillet. Stir in the cauliflower once the butter has melted, adding more as necessary. Cook without the lid for 10-15 minutes until soft, stirring frequently. stir in the cheese.

Nutrition Information

Calories 86, Fat 6.9 g , Total Carbohydrate 5.1g, Total Sugars 2.3g , Protein 2.4g, Potassium 292 mg, Sodium 84 mg

Storage: a sealed container is used to store Garlic Asiago Cauliflower Rice for up to 3 -4 days

Reheat: just defrost at room temperature for a few hours

11.3 Maple-Roasted Sweet Potatoes

Preparation: 15 minutes
Cooking time 1 hr.10 minutes
Servings: 12

Ingredients

- butter, melted -2 tbsp.- 30 g
- salt -½ tsp. – 2 g
- lemon juice -1 tbsp.- 15 ml
- Freshly ground pepper, to taste
- pure maple syrup -⅓ cup – 105g
- sweet potatoes, peeled and cut -2 1/2 pounds – 1.1kg

Preparation

1. heating oven to 400°F (204 C).
2. Arrange sweet potatoes in a 9 by 13-inch baking dish in an equal layer. In a small bowl, mix the butter, maple syrup, lemon juice, salt, and pepper. The sweet potatoes are then tossed in the mixture after being poured over.
3. Cover the sweet potatoes and bake them for 15 minutes. Remove the top, mix the food, and boil it for a further 45 to 50 minutes when it's soft and beginning to brown.

Nutrition Information

Calories 152, Fat 2.1 g, Total Carbohydrate 32.3g, Total Sugars 5.7g, Protein 1.5g, Potassium 791 mg, Sodium 120 mg
Storage:a sealed container is used to store Maple-Roasted Sweet Potatoes for up to 3 -4 days
Reheat: just defrost at room temperature for a few hours

11.4 Parmesan Potato Wedges

Preparation: 10 minutes
Cooking time 20 minutes
Servings: 8

Ingredients

- medium baking potatoes (about 8 ounces each) – 4
- grated Parmesan cheese – ¼ cup – 4 g
- paprika -1/2 tsp.- 2 g
- garlic salt -1 tsp.-4 g
- garlic powder -1/2 tsp.- 2 g
- Cooking spray
- dried oregano -1/2 tsp.- 2 g
-

Preparation

1. Turn the oven to 400 degrees (204 C). Combine the first five components.
2. Arrange each potato, cut lengthwise into eight wedges, in a parchment-lined 15x10x1-inch baking dish. Cooking spray should be used before scattering the cheese mixture. 30 minutes or until tender in the oven.

Nutrition Information

Calories 70, Fat 0.4 g , Total Carbohydrate 15.8g, Total Sugars 0.7g, Protein 2.1g, Potassium 371 mg, Sodium 17 mg
Storage:a sealed container is used to store Parmesan Potato Wedges for up to 3 -4 days
Reheat: just defrost at room temperature for a few hours

11.5 Roasted Garlic-Parmesan Cabbage

Preparation: 10 minutes
Cooking time 30 minutes
Servings: 8

Ingredients

- salt -½ tsp.-2 g
- rice vinegar-3 tbsp.-45 ml
- extra-virgin olive oil -3 tbsp.-45 ml
- cloves garlic, finely minced or grated -4 medium
- crushed red pepper flakes (optional) -¼ tsp.- 1 g
- reduced-sodium soy sauce 1 tbsp. -15 ml

- head red or green cabbage -½ large
- grated Parmesan cheese -6 tbsp- 90 g

Preparation

1. Set the oven to 425°F (218°C). Keep the core in tact when cutting the cabbage into 8 wedges, each about one inch broad.
2. In a small bowl, mix the Parmesan, garlic, oil, vinegar, soy sauce, and salt. Place the cabbage wedges on a big rimmed baking sheet, cut-side down. Garlic-Parmesan mixture should be applied to the cabbage's entire surface. About 20 minutes of roasting should produce golden brown edges. For an additional 10 minutes, flip the cabbage and roast it until it is soft and brown. If desired, add some Parmesan cheese and/or crushed red pepper.

Nutrition Information

Calories 139, Fat 9.9 g, Total Carbohydrate 6g, Total Sugars 2.5g , Protein 8g, Potassium 144 mg, Sodium 432 mg

Storage:a sealed container is used to store Roasted Garlic-Parmesan Cabbage for up to 3 - 4 days

Reheat: just defrost at room temperature for a few hours

11.6 Zesty Garlic Green Beans

Preparation: 15 minutes
Cooking time 10 minutes
Servings: 10

Ingredients

- oil from oil-packed sun-dried tomatoes -2 tbsp.-30 ml
- garlic cloves, minced -3
- frozen french-style green beans -2 packages (16 ounces each) -900 g
- oil-packed sun-dried tomatoes, chopped -1/2 cup – 55 g
- lemon-pepper seasoning -1-1/2 tsp. – 6g
- sliced sweet onion -1 cup -115 g

Preparation

1. Heat the oil in a Dutch oven over medium heat. For three to four minutes, or until the onion is soft, sauté and toss the onion. Cook and stir for a further 2 minutes after adding the tomatoes, garlic, and lemon pepper.
2. Add frozen green beans and cook thoroughly for 7-9 minutes with a cover on. Remove the lid after the liquid has almost all evaporated, then simmer for a further two to three minutes.

Nutrition Information

Calories 21, Fat 1 g, Total Carbohydrate 3 g , Total Sugars 0.6g, Protein 0.6g, Potassium 109 mg, Sodium 34 mg

Storage:a sealed container is used to store Zesty Garlic Green Beans for up to 3 -4 days

Reheat: just defrost at room temperature for a few hours

11.7 Balsamic Oven-Roasted Carrots

Preparation: 10 minutes
Cooking time 30 minutes
Servings: 4

Ingredients

- balsamic vinegar - 2 tbsp. – 30 ml
- carrots, preferably multicolour, -1 pound -450 g
- olive oil, divided - 2 tbsp. – 30 ml
- pure maple syrup -1 tbsp. -15 g
- toasted hazelnuts (Optional) - 2 tbsp. – 30 g
- salt -¼ tsp.- 1g

Preparation

1. Heat the oven to 400 degrees Fahrenheit (204 C). In a small bowl, mix the vinegar, maple syrup, and 1 tbsp. oil.
2. Add the carrots, salt, and remaining 1 tablespoon oil to a large basin and toss

to coat. On a baking sheet with a rim, spread out in a single layer.

3. Roast the carrots for 16 to 18 minutes, or until they are starting to colour and are tender but not quite cooked through. Use a spatula to properly spread the carrots with the balsamic mixture after drizzling it over them. Roast the carrots for an additional 5 minutes or so, or until they are coated and fork-tender. If desired, sprinkle some toasted hazelnuts on top. Serve immediately.

Nutrition Information

Calories 136, Fat 8.4 g, Total Carbohydrate 15g, Total Sugars 8.7g , Protein 1.4g, Potassium 394 mg, Sodium 226 mg

Storage:a sealed container is used to store Balsamic Oven-Roasted Carrots for up to 3 -4 days

Reheat: just defrost at room temperature for a few hours

11.8 Red Potatoes with Beans

Preparation: 10 minutes

Cooking time 10 minutes

Servings: 6

Ingredients

- chopped red onion -1/2 cup – 56 g
- fresh green beans, trimmed -1-1/3 pounds – 600 g
- red potatoes, cut into wedges -6 small
- Italian salad dressing -1/2 cup – 117 g

Preparation

1. Fill a big saucepan with water, then add the potatoes. boiling level Covered, simmer for 10 to 15 minutes or until fork-tender. Warm up less.
2. Put green beans with just enough water to cover them in a 2-quart microwave-safe dish. Microwave covered for 6 to 8 minutes on high until tender. Place the washed potatoes and beans in a bowl. Combine the onion and dressing.

Nutrition Information

Calories 203, Fat 5.9 g, Total Carbohydrate 35.4g, Total Sugars 4.8g, Protein 4.8g, Potassium 955 mg, Sodium 21 mg

Storage:a sealed container is used to store Red Potatoes with Beans for up to 3 -4 days

Reheat: just defrost at room temperature for a few hours

11.9 Lemon Couscous with Broccoli

Preparation: 15 minutes

Cooking time 10 minutes

Servings: 6

Ingredients

- salt -1/2 tsp.- 2g
- olive oil -1 tbsp.-15 ml
- fresh broccoli florets, cut into small pieces -4 cups – 400 g
- Coarsely ground pepper-1/4 tsp.- 1g
- dried basil-1/2 tsp.- 2g
- grated lemon zest -1 tsp.-4g
- reduced-sodium chicken broth -1-1/4 cups – 300 ml
- slivered almonds, toasted-1 tbsp.- 15g
- Garlic cloves, minced -2
- uncooked whole wheat couscous -1 cup – 56 g
- lemon juice-1 tsp.-4ml

Preparation

1. Heat oil over medium-high heat in a sizable cast-iron pan or other large skillet. Broccoli should be stir-fried until crisp-tender along with the other ingredients.
2. You can add garlic and couscous. Cook and toss for a further 1-2 minutes. Add the seasonings, broth, lemon juice, and zest, and bring to a boil. Turn off the heat, cover the pan, and let the broth sit for 5 to 10 minutes. With a fork, fluff. Almonds should be topped.

Nutrition Information

Calories 170, Fat 4.3 g, Total Carbohydrate 28.8g, Total Sugars 1.5g, Protein 7.8g, Potassium 240 mg, Sodium 341 mg

Storage: a sealed container is used to store Lemon Couscous with Broccoli for up to 3 -4 days

Reheat: just defrost at room temperature for a few hours

11.10 Roasted Squash with Garlic & Parsley

Preparation: 15 minutes

Cooking time 10 minutes

Servings: 10

Ingredients

- salt -1 ½ tsp.-6g
- extra-virgin olive oil, divided -2 tbsp.- 30 ml
- garlic, minced -3 cloves
- winter squash-5 pounds -2.2kg
- freshly ground pepper, divided -¼ tsp. 1g
- chopped Italian parsley -2 tbsp.-7g

Preparation

1. Warm the oven to 375°F (190°C).
2. Combine the squash with 1/4 teaspoon each of salt, pepper, and 4 teaspoons of oil. Spread it evenly across a sizable baking sheet. Roast for 30 to 45 minutes, tossing regularly, or until softly browned and uniformly cooked (depending on the variety of squash).
3. In a little saucepan set over medium heat, warm the 2 tablespoons of remaining oil. When the garlic is fragrant but not browned, add it and simmer, stirring regularly, for 30 to 60 seconds. Roasted butternut squash, parsley, and garlic should all be combined. flavouring, serving, and tasting come next.

Nutrition Information

Calories 116, Fat 3 g, Total Carbohydrate 24g, Total Sugars 0g, Protein 1.9g, Potassium 795 mg, Sodium 7 mg

Storage: a sealed container is used to store Roasted Squash with Garlic & Parsley for up to 3 -4 days

Reheat: just defrost at room temperature for a few hours

12 POULTRY RECIPES

12.1 Tropical Chicken Cauliflower Rice Bowls

Preparation: 40 minutes

Cooking time 10 minutes

Servings: 4

Ingredients

- boneless skinless chicken breast halves (6 ounces each) – 4- 680 g
- pineapple, peeled, cored and cubed -1 fresh -495 g
- chili powder -1/8 tsp.
- lime juice, divided -3 tbsp.-45 ml
- Optional: Toasted sweetened shredded coconut or lime wedges
- canola oil -1 tbsp.-15 ml
- fresh cauliflower florets -3 cups – 300 g
- crushed red pepper flakes -1/4 tsp.-1 g
- fresh cilantro, divided -2 tablespoons plus 1/2 cup chopped -20 g
- plain or coconut Greek yogurt -1/2 cup – 85 g
- salt, divided -3/4 tsp.-3g
- red onion, finely chopped -1 small

Preparation

1. Combine 1 cup pineapple, yoghurt, 2 tablespoons of cilantro and lime juice, and 1/4 teaspoon of each salt, pepper flakes, and chilli powder in a food processor to prepare the marinade. In a

large bowl, toss the chicken with the marinade; cover and chill for 1-3 hours.

2. A clean food processor should be used to prepare cauliflower until it resembles rice (do not over-process). In a sizable skillet, heat the oil over medium-high heat. The onion should be sautéed for three to five minutes, until just lightly browned. After adding, stir-fry the cauliflower for 5–7 minutes, or until just barely browned. Stir in 1/2 teaspoon salt, 1 tablespoon of the remaining lime juice, and 1 cup of pineapple. Cook cauliflower for 3 to 5 minutes, covered, over medium heat, or until tender. The last 1/2 cup of cilantro should be added. Keep warm.

3. Turn on the broiler or grill. Drain the chicken, then discard the marinade. Put the chicken on a grill rack over medium heat, in a 15x10x1-inch oiled pan, or both. 4 inches from the heat, grill, cover, or broil for 4-6 minutes on each side, or until an instant-read thermometer reads 165°. You should wait five minutes before slicing.

4. Before serving, divide the cauliflower mixture among 4 bowls. On top, place the chicken, the remaining cup of pineapple, and, if desired, the lime and coconut wedges.

Nutrition Information
Calories 385, Fat 15.1 g, Total Carbohydrate 17.6g, Total Sugars 8.6g, Protein 45g , Potassium 825 mg, Sodium 617 mg

Storage: a sealed container is used to store Tropical Chicken Cauliflower Rice Bowls for up to 3 -4 days

Reheat: just defrost at room temperature for a few hours

12.2 Chicken-Noodle Casserole
Preparation: 15 minutes
Cooking time 1hr. 10 minutes
Servings: 8

Ingredients
- flour -2 tbsp. -30 g
- salt -¾ tsp. 3g
- dried thyme, crushed -1 tsp.-4g
- snipped fresh parsley -2 tbsp.-6g
- Celery, chopped (2 cups) -4 stalks – 160 g
- canola oil -2 tsp. – 8 ml
- bread -1 slice
- jumbo or extra-large egg noodles -10 ounces – 280 g
- light sour cream -1 (8 ounce) carton - 226 g
- onion, chopped (1/2 cup) -1 medium
- garlic powder -½ tsp. -2 g
- chicken legs and/or thighs, skinned -2 pounds -900g
- black pepper -½ tsp.-2g
- water -6 cups – 1.4 L
- Cooking spray

Preparation
1. The oven should be preheated at 375 degrees. In a Dutch oven, sauté the onion and celery for three minutes at medium heat while stirring occasionally. Add the chicken, pepper, thyme, and salt to a Dutch oven. For two minutes, cook. Add the water. After boiling, heat should be lowered. After 20 to 25 minutes of cooking, the chicken shouldn't be pink. covered

2. For the topping, rip the bread into little pieces. Finely chop the remaining celery and onion. Place the bread, onion, and celery in a small bowl and toss to combine.

3. Using a slotted spoon, transfer the chicken to a cutting board so it can cool a little. The noodles should be cooked, frequently tossing, for 7 to 8 minutes, or until just soft, in a Dutch oven with simmering stock. Using a slotted spoon, transfer the noodles, celery, and onion to a 3-quart baking dish.

4. In a bowl, mix the sour cream, flour, and garlic powder to form the sauce. Whisk in 1 cup of the heated broth gradually until smooth. Stir the sour cream mixture in when the broth in the Dutch oven is boiling.

5. Remove the chicken from the bones and discard them. To the noodles in the baking dish, add chopped chicken. Slowly incorporate sauce. A little coating of frying spray should be applied before adding the bread topping.

6. Bake for 30 to 35 minutes, uncovered, or until topping begins to brown and food is fully warmed. Add parsley as a garnish just before serving.

Nutrition Information

Calories 353, Fat 16.4 g, Total Carbohydrate 14.1 g, Total Sugars 1g, Protein 35.6g, Potassium 385 mg, Sodium 352 mg

Storage: a sealed container is used to store Chicken-Noodle Casserole for up to 3 -4 days

Reheat: just defrost at room temperature for a few hours

12.3 Spicy Chicken Pumpkin Pizza

Preparation: 15 minutes
Cooking time 10 minutes
Servings: 2

Ingredients

- mild chunky salsa - 1/2 cup – 100 g
- cubed cooked chicken -1-1/2 cups – 210 g
- Minced fresh cilantro, optional
- salt -1/4 tsp.-1 g
- chipotle peppers in adobo sauce, minced -2
- olive oil -1 tbsp. -15 ml
- canned pumpkin -3/4 cup – 190 g
- shredded part-skim mozzarella cheese - 1-1/2 cups -45 g
- pepper -1/8 tsp.

- frozen cauliflower pizza crust or 2 prebaked 12-inch thin whole wheat pizza crusts -2 packages (7-1/2 ounces each) – 452 g
- red onion -1/4 cup – 28 g

Preparation

1. Set the oven's temperature to 375 degrees. In a Dutch oven, sauté the onion and celery for three minutes at medium heat while stirring occasionally. Add the chicken, pepper, thyme, and salt to a Dutch oven. For two minutes, cook. Add the water. After boiling, heat should be lowered. After 20 to 25 minutes of cooking under a covered dish, the chicken should no longer be pink.

2. To prepare the topping, rip the bread into little pieces. Finely chop the remaining celery and onion. Place the bread, onion, and celery in a small bowl and toss to combine.

3. Using a slotted spoon, transfer the chicken to a cutting board so it can cool a little. The noodles should be cooked, tossing frequently, for 7 to 8 minutes, or until just soft, in a Dutch oven with simmering stock. Using a slotted spoon, transfer the noodles, celery, and onion to a 3-quart baking dish.

4. In a bowl, mix the sour cream, flour, and garlic powder to form the sauce. Whisk in 1 cup of the heated broth gradually until smooth. Stir the sour cream mixture in when the broth in the Dutch oven is boiling.

5. Remove the chicken from the bones and discard them. To the noodles in the baking dish, add chopped chicken. Slowly incorporate sauce. A little coating of frying spray should be applied before adding the bread topping.

6. Bake for 30 to 35 minutes, uncovered, or until topping begins to brown and

food is fully warmed. Add parsley as a garnish just before serving.

Nutrition Information

Calories 493, Fat 23.9 g, Total Carbohydrate 38.3g, Total Sugars 6.7g, Protein 35.6g, Potassium 352 mg, Sodium 666 mg

Storage:a sealed container is used to store Spicy Chicken Pumpkin Pizza for up to 3 -4 days

Reheat: just defrost at room temperature for a few hours

12.4 Lemon Chicken & Potatoes with Kale

Preparation: 15 minutes
Cooking time 30 minutes
Servings: 4

Ingredients

- garlic, minced -4 cloves
- chopped fresh tarragon -1 tbsp -3 g
- baby kale -6 cups -510 g
- boneless, skinless chicken thighs, trimmed -1 pound – 450 g
- chicken broth -½ cup – 120 ml
- extra-virgin olive oil, divided -3 tbsp. – 45 ml
- baby Yukon Gold potatoes, halved lengthwise -1 pound – 450 g
- salt, divided -½ tsp.-2 g
- ground pepper, divided-½ tsp.-2 g
- lemon, sliced and seeds removed -1 large

Preparation

1. heat oven to 400°F (204°C).
2. Warm 1 tablespoon of oil in a big cast-iron pan over medium-high heat. Sprinkle the chicken with 1/4 tablespoons of salt and pepper. Cook, flipping once, for about 5 minutes total, or until both sides are browned. Put thereon a plate.
3. Add the remaining 2 tablespoons of oil, the potatoes, and the final 1/4 teaspoon of salt to the pan. Cook the potatoes for 3 minutes, or until golden,

cut-side down. Stir in the tarragon, lemon, garlic, and broth. Re-add the chicken to the pan.
4. Position the pan in the oven. The chicken should roast for about 15 minutes, or until it is fully cooked. When the kale has wilted, add it to the mixture and roast for 3 to 4 minutes.

Nutrition Information

Calories 496, Fat 19.6 g, Total Carbohydrate 43.8g , Total Sugars 1.7g, Protein 39.7g, Potassium 1140 mg, Sodium 444 mg

Storage:a sealed container is used to store Lemon Chicken & Potatoes with Kale for up to 3 -4 days

Reheat: just defrost at room temperature for a few hours

12.5 Autumn Apple Chicken

Preparation: 25 minutes
Cooking time 20 minutes
Servings: 4

Ingredients

- Fuji or Gala apples, coarsely chopped - 2 medium
- barbecue sauce -1/3 cup- 62 g
- apple cider or juice -1/2 cup – 120 ml
- honey -1 tbsp.- 15 g
- pepper1/4 tsp.-1g
- canola oil -1 tbsp. – 15 ml
- salt -1/4 tsp.-1g
- garlic clove, minced - 1
- onion, chopped -1 medium
- bone-in chicken thighs (about 1-1/2 pounds), skin removed -4

Preparation

1. Salt and pepper should be added to chicken. Select the saute or browning setting on a 6-qt. electric pressure cooker. Add oil and set the heat to medium. The chicken should be cooked in the hot oil, then taken out and kept warm.

2. Add cider and whisk to scrape up any browned bits from the pan. Chicken, onion, honey, garlic, and barbecue sauce should all be added. Choose "cancel." Lock the lid and close the pressure-release valve. Prepare for high pressure cooking for 10 minutes. Five minutes should pass naturally before relieving any pressure that still remains. At least 170 degrees should be recorded on a chicken thermometer.

3. After removal, keep the chicken warm. Reduce the heat and select the saute option. Cook for 10 minutes with frequent stirring after adding the apples. serving it with chicken

Nutrition Information
Calories 380, Fat 20.9 g, Total Carbohydrate 26.4g, Total Sugars 21.3g, Protein 20.5g, Potassium 188 mg, Sodium 468 mg
Storage: a sealed container is used to store Autumn Apple Chicken for up to 3 -4 days
Reheat: just defrost at room temperature for a few hours

12.6 Chicken Tetrazzini

Preparation: 15 minutes
Cooking time 10 minutes
Servings: 6
Ingredients
- fine dry breadcrumbs -¼ cup – 30 g
- canola oil -2 tsp. -8 ml
- leeks, white parts only, -3
- button mushrooms, quartered -6 ounces – 170 g
- finely chopped fresh parsley -1 tbsp.-3g
- reduced-sodium chicken broth -3 cups – 720 ml
- cubed cooked chicken breast -2 cups – 280 g
- Grated zest of 1 lemon
- freshly grated Parmesan cheese -⅓ cup – 9 g
- fettuccine, preferably spinach -6 ounces – 170 g
- Lemon juice, to taste
- low-fat milk -½ cup – 120 ml
- all-purpose flour -3 tbsp. – 45 g
- Salt & freshly ground pepper, to taste
- chopped fresh rosemary, divided -1 tsp.- 4 g

Preparation
1. Set oven to 425 degrees Fahrenheit (218C). Spray cooking oil in a 3-quart baking pan.
2. Cook fettuccine in salted boiling water for 8 minutes or until al dente. Drain, then rehydrate with running cold water. Drain, and then separate.
3. Heat some oil in a large skillet over medium heat in the meanwhile. Leeks must be added, then cooked for 6 to 8 minutes with constant stirring. Stir-fry the mushrooms for about 5 minutes, or until they are cooked through, along with 1/2 teaspoon rosemary. Add the flour and whisk for one minute. Cook over high heat for 4 more minutes, stirring often, until somewhat thickened. Add milk and broth. Add the chicken after turning the heat off. Season with salt, pepper, and lemon juice.
4. Before spooning the chicken mixture into the baking dish, gently stir the cooked fettuccine into the chicken mixture.
5. In a separate bowl, mix the Parmesan, breadcrumbs, lemon zest, and parsley with the remaining 1/2 teaspoon of rosemary. To taste, add salt and pepper. The mixture will be spread over the casserole.
6. Bake casserole for 20 to 30 minutes, or until bubbling. Allow to stand for five minutes before serving.

Nutrition Information
Calories 267, Fat 5.4 g, Total Carbohydrate 31.1g, Total Sugars 4.2g, Protein 23g, Potassium 463 mg, Sodium 541 mg

Storage: a sealed container is used to store Chicken Tetrazzini for up to 3 -4 days

Reheat: just defrost at room temperature for a few hours

12.7 Chicken & Asparagus Bake

Preparation: 15 minutes

Cooking time 35 minutes

Servings: 4

Ingredients

- salt, divided -¾ tsp. – 3 g
- ground coriander, divided -2 tsp.-8 g
- lemon juice -2 tbsp. -30 ml
- baby Yukon Gold potatoes, halved lengthwise -12 ounces -340 g
- boneless, skinless chicken breasts, cut in half crosswise -2 (8 ounce) -450 g
- whole-grain Dijon mustard -1 tbsp. -15 g
- chopped shallot -2 tbsp. .- 30 g
- carrots, diagonally sliced into 1-inch pieces -8 ounces -226 g
- honey -2 tsp.-8g
- ground pepper, divided -½ tsp. – 2 g
- chopped fresh dill -1 tbsp.-3 g
- Lemon wedges
- extra-virgin olive oil, divided -3 tbsp. – 45 ml
- chopped fresh flat-leaf parsley -2 tbsp.-6 g
- fresh asparagus, trimmed -1 pound – 450 g

Preparation

1. Turn on the 375°F (190°C) oven. Put the chicken on a spotless work surface and wrap it in plastic.
2. Pound the chicken pieces to a uniform thickness of 1/2 inch using a meat mallet.
3. Arrange on a big baking sheet with a rim on one side.
4. Arrange the potatoes and carrots on the other half of the pan in a single layer.
5. Toss the chicken and veggies with 1 tablespoon of oil, 1 teaspoon of coriander, 1/2 teaspoon of salt, and 1/4 teaspoon of pepper.
6. A 15-minute baking period.
7. In the meantime, combine the lemon juice, shallot, mustard, honey, and other seasonings in a small bowl with the remaining 2 tablespoons oil, 1 teaspoon coriander, 1/4 teaspoon salt, and 1/4 teaspoon pepper.
8. Remove the pan from the oven and turn on the broiler.
9. After stirring the potato-carrot mixture, add the asparagus to the centre of the pan.
10. Evenly distribute the lemon juice-shallot mixture over the chicken and vegetables.
11. Broil the chicken for about 10 minutes, or until it registers 165°F on an instant-read thermometer, the vegetables are crisp-tender, and the chicken is lightly browned.
12. After removing from the oven, evenly distribute the parsley and dill. Lemon wedges are recommended.

Nutrition Information

Calories 436, Fat 19.9 g, Total Carbohydrate 28.4g, Total Sugars 9.1g, Protein 37.7g, Potassium 1108 mg, Sodium 657 mg

Storage: a sealed container is used to store Chicken & Asparagus Bake for up to 3 -4 days

Reheat: just defrost at room temperature for a few hours

12.8 Chicken and Broccoli with Dill Sauce

Preparation: 15 minutes

Cooking time 15 minutes

Servings: 4

Ingredients

- chicken broth -1 cup – 240 ml
- Pepper -1/4 tsp. – 1 g
- boneless skinless chicken breast halves (6 ounces each) - 4
- fresh broccoli florets - 4 cups – 360 g

- olive oil-1 tbsp.-15 ml
- snipped fresh dill -1 tbsp.-3 g
- all-purpose flour -1 tbsp.-15 g
- garlic salt -1/2 tsp.-2 g
- 2% milk -1 cup – 240 ml

Preparation

1. Season the chicken with salt, pepper, and garlic. In oil that has been heated in a large skillet over medium heat, cook the chicken on all sides. Take the pan out.
2. The broccoli and broth should be cooked in the same skillet. Reduce heat; cover and cook broccoli for three to five minutes, or until just tender. With a slotted spoon, remove the broccoli from the pan while saving the broth. Cook the broccoli.
3. Combine flour, milk, and dill in a small basin; add to the pan of broth. Bring to a boil while constantly stirring; cook and stir for 1-2 minutes, or until thickened. The chicken should be added, covered, and cooked for 10–12 minutes, or until the internal temperature reaches 165°F (74°C). serve alongside broccoli.

Nutrition Information

Calories 389, Fat 16.3 g, Total Carbohydrate 11.5g, Total Sugars 4.6g, Protein 48.4g, Potassium 763 mg, Sodium 377 mg

Storage: a sealed container is used to store Chicken and Broccoli with Dill Sauce for up to 3 -4 days

Reheat: just defrost at room temperature for a few hours

12.9 Roast Chicken & Sweet Potato

Preparation: 15 minutes
Cooking time 10 minutes
Servings: 4

Ingredients

- salt, divided -½ tsp. – 2 g
- chicken thighs, -1 1/2-2 pounds -900g
- red onion, cut into 1-inch wedges -1 large
- chopped fresh thyme -2 tbsp. – 6 g
- extra-virgin olive oil, divided -2 tbsp. – 30 ml
- whole-grain or Dijon mustard -2 tbsp. – 30 g
- freshly ground pepper, divided --½ tsp. – 2 g
- sweet potatoes, peeled and cut into 1-inch pieces -2 medium

Preparation

1. Position the oven rack in the bottom third and heat it to 450 degrees Fahrenheit (232C). Place a large baking sheet with a rim inside the oven and preheat it.
2. In a small dish, combine the mustard, thyme, 1 tablespoon oil, and 1/4 teaspoon each of salt and pepper. Apply the mixture evenly on the chicken after that.
3. To the bowl containing the sweet potatoes and onion, add the remaining 1 tablespoon of oil, 1/4 teaspoon of salt, and 1/4 teaspoon of pepper. Carefully take the baking sheet out of the oven and spread the vegetables on it. Place the chicken on top of the vegetables.
4. Place the pan back in the oven and roast for an additional 30 to 35 minutes, or until the veggies are tender and beginning to brown and an instant-read thermometer inserted into a chicken thigh registers 165 degrees F.

Nutrition Information

Calories 532, Fat 33.1 g, Total Carbohydrate 25.4g, Total Sugars 2g, Protein 32.1g, Potassium 688 mg, Sodium 517 mg

Storage: a sealed container is used to store Roast Chicken & Sweet Potato for up to 3 -4 days

Reheat: just defrost at room temperature for a few hours

12.10 Red Pepper Chicken

Preparation: 15 minutes

Cooking time 10 minutes

Servings: 4

Ingredients

- roasted sweet red peppers, drained and cut into strips -1 jar (12 ounces) -340 g
- onion, chopped -1 large
- skinless chicken breast halves (4 ounces each) -4 boneless
- Pepper to taste
- no-salt-added black beans, rinsed and drained -1 can (15 ounces) -425 g
- Hot cooked rice
- Mexican stewed tomatoes, undrained -1 can (14-1/2 ounces) -410 g
- water -1/2 cup -120 ml

Preparation

1. In a 6-qt. electric pressure cooker, add the chicken. Beans, tomatoes, red peppers, onions, water, and pepper are combined in a bowl and then poured over the chicken. Close the pressure-release valve and lock the lid. Adapt to pressure-cook for 5 minutes on high.
2. Rapidly releasing pressure. Select "cancel." Chicken should have a thermometer inserted at least 165 degrees. Keep chicken warm after removing it. Choose the saute option and lower the heat. Cooking liquids should be simmered for 8–10 minutes to thicken. Serve alongside chicken and rice.

Nutrition Information

Calories 458, Fat 15.3 g, Total Carbohydrate 28.9g, Total Sugars 8.8g, Protein 50.6g, Potassium 1153 mg, Sodium 658 mg

Storage: a sealed container is used to store Red Pepper Chicken for up to 3 -4 days

Reheat: just defrost at room temperature for a few hours

12.11 Red Beans and Rice with Chicken

Preparation: 05 minutes

Cooking time 20 minutes

Servings: 4

Ingredients

- garlic, minced -2 cloves
- coarsely chopped green sweet pepper (1 medium) -¾ cup – 111 g
- ground black pepper-¼ tsp.- 1g
- olive oil -1 tbsp.-15 ml
- skinless, boneless chicken breast, cut into 1-inch pieces -10 ounces -280 g
- salt -¼ tsp.- 1g
- ready-to-serve cooked brown rice,- 1 container – 200 g
- red beans, rinsed and drained -1 (15 ounce) can -425 g
- 1 pinch Cayenne pepper
- reduced-sodium chicken broth -¼ cup – 60 ml
- ground cumin -½ tsp. – 2 g
- chopped onion (1 medium) -½ cup – 58 g
- cayenne pepper -½ tsp. – 2 g
- Lime wedges

Preparation

1. Season the chicken with salt and black pepper. In a large skillet, heat oil to medium-high heat. Add the chicken, sweet pepper, onion, and garlic when the chicken is no longer pink and the vegetables are cooked. For 8 to 10 minutes, cook and stir.
2. Combine the chicken mixture with the beans, rice, broth, cumin, and 1/4 teaspoon cayenne pepper in the skillet. Warm thru. Lime slices are not required. If desired, add extra cayenne pepper.

Nutrition Information

Calories 266, Fat 6.9 g, Total Carbohydrate 29.3g, Total Sugars 3.4g, Protein 23.1g, Potassium 393 mg, Sodium 497 mg

Storage: a sealed container is used to store Red Beans and Rice with Chicken for up to 3 -4 days

Reheat: just defrost at room temperature for a few hours

12.12 Parmesan Chicken with Artichoke Hearts

Preparation: 20 minutes

Cooking time 20 minutes

Servings: 4

Ingredients

- dried rosemary, crushed -1 tsp.-4 g
- dried thyme -1/2 tsp.-2 g
- 1 lemon, cut into 8 slices
- pepper-1/2 tsp.-2 g
- olive oil, divided -3 tsp. -12 ml
- skinless chicken breast halves (6 ounces each) -4 boneless (170 g each)
- 2 green onions, thinly sliced
- chicken broth -1/2 cup – 120 ml
- Artichoke hearts, 2 cans (14 ounces each) -700 g
- garlic cloves, chopped - 2
- onion, coarsely chopped -1 medium
- shredded Parmesan cheese -1/4 cup – 7 g

Preparation

1. Set the oven to 375 degrees (190 C). Cooking spray-coated 15x10x1-inch baking pan: Add chicken; add 1-1/2 teaspoons oil. Combine rosemary, thyme, and pepper in a small bowl; sprinkle half over chicken.

2. In a large bowl, combine and coat the artichoke hearts with the remaining herb combination, onion, wine, garlic, and oil. encircle the chicken with. The chicken with the cheese topping is garnished with lemon wedges.

3. Roast for 20 to 25 minutes, or until the chicken reaches 165 degrees on an instant-read thermometer. Top with some green onions.

Nutrition Information

Calories 397, Fat 15 g , Total Carbohydrate 14.8g, Total Sugars 2.8g, Protein 46.2g, Potassium 778 mg, Sodium 223 mg

Storage: a sealed container is used to store Parmesan Chicken with Artichoke Hearts for up to 3 -4 days

Reheat: just defrost at room temperature for a few hours

12.13 Cauliflower Chicken Fried "Rice"

Preparation: 15 minutes

Cooking time 20 minutes

Servings: 4

Ingredients

- grated fresh ginger -1 tbsp.-15 g
- eggs, beaten -2 large
- sesame oil (optional) -1 tsp – 4 ml
- reduced-sodium tamari -3 tbsp. – 45 ml
- boneless, skinless chicken thighs, trimmed and cut into 1/2-inch pieces - 1 pound – 450 g
- peanut oil, divided (1 tsp.+2 tbsp.) –(4 ml +30 ml)
- minced garlic-1 tbsp.-15 g
- cauliflower rice -4 cups – 400 g
- diced red bell pepper -½ cup – 75 g
- Scallions, thinly sliced, whites and greens separated - 3
- snow peas, trimmed and halved -1 cup -160 g

Preparation

1. Heat 1 teaspoon oil in a sizable flat-bottomed carbon steel wok or heavy pan over high heat. The eggs should be added and fried for around 30 seconds, merely flipping them once and without stirring. Fry the other side for a further 15 seconds, or until just cooked. Move

to a cutting board and then cut into 1/2-inch pieces.

2. Add 1 tablespoon of oil to the pan along with the scallion whites, ginger, and garlic. Cook for 30 seconds, stirring constantly, or until the scallions are soft. Add the chicken and stir for 1 minute. Add the bell pepper and snow peas; cook for 2 to 4 minutes, stirring occasionally, until just tender. Stack everything onto a large plate.

3. For about 2 minutes, or until the cauliflower rice begins to soften, stir the remaining 1 tablespoon oil into the pan with the cauliflower rice.

4. Add the tamari and sesame oil after adding the chicken mixture and eggs back to the pan (if using). Scallion greens can be added as a garnish.

Nutrition Information

Calories 293, Fat 12.2 g, Total Carbohydrate 11.4g, Total Sugars 5.7g, Protein 34g, Potassium 413mg, Sodium 747 mg

Storage:a sealed container is used to store Cauliflower Chicken Fried "Rice" for up to 3 -4 days

Reheat: just defrost at room temperature for a few hours

12.14 Maple-Glazed Chicken Breasts

Preparation: 15 minutes

Cooking time 10 minutes

Servings: 2

Ingredients

- minced fresh ginger -1 tsp.-4 g
- chicken breasts, (about 8 ounces), trimmed and tenders removed -2 (226 g)
- lemon juice -2 tsp.-8 ml
- garlic, minced -1 clove
- pure maple syrup -2 tbsp.-30 ml
- reduced-sodium soy sauce -1 tbsp. – 15 ml
- freshly ground pepper -¼ tsp.-1 g

Preparation

1. In a small, shallow dish, mix the pepper, ginger, garlic lemon juice, soy sauce, and syrup. After rotating the chicken to coat it completely with the marinade, add the chicken. During the two hours of chilling under cover, the chicken was turned once.

2. Before heating an indoor grill pan, spray it with cooking spray. Remove the chicken from the marinade and cook for 4 minutes on each side until the thickest part of the breast registers 165 degrees F on an instant-read thermometer.

3. During this time, boil the leftover marinade in a small pot. Cook for around 4 minutes, or until the reduction has decreased by about half. Serve the chicken with a generous coating of the thickened reduced sauce.

Nutrition Information

Calories 342, Fat 11 g , Total Carbohydrate 15.6g, Total Sugars 12.2g, Protein 43g, Potassium 439 mg, Sodium 429 mg

Storage:a sealed container is used to store Maple-Glazed Chicken Breasts for up to 3 -4 days

Reheat: just defrost at room temperature for a few hours

12.15 Easy Caribbean Chicken

Preparation: 10 minutes

Cooking time 10 minutes

Servings: 4

Ingredients

- olive oil -1 tbsp. – 15 ml
- barbecue sauce -1/4 cup – 62 g
- chicken breasts, -1 pound – 450 g
- fire-roasted diced tomatoes -1 can (14-1/2 ounces) -410 g
- Fresh cilantro leaves, optional
- Hot cooked rice
- garlic-herb seasoning blend -2 tsp.- 8 g

- unsweetened pineapple chunks -1 can (8 ounces) -226 g

Preparation

1. Put a large nonstick skillet on medium-high heat. The chicken should be barely browned and no longer pink after about 5 minutes of cooking, flipping it once or twice. Inputs include tomato, pineapple, and barbecue sauce. Cook and stir for 5-7 minutes after coming to a boil, or until flavours are incorporated and chicken is cooked through. If desired, serve over rice and fresh cilantro.

Nutrition Information

Calories 296, Fat 12 g , Total Carbohydrate 14.1g, Total Sugars 8.9g, Protein 33.3g, Potassium 353 mg, Sodium 335 mg

Storage:a sealed container is used to store Easy Caribbean Chicken for up to 3 -4 days

Reheat: just defrost at room temperature for a few hours

13 LEAN BEEF RECIPES

13.1 Greek Sloppy Joes

Preparation: 10 minutes
Cooking time 25 minutes
Servings: 6

Ingredients

- garlic cloves, minced -2
- kaiser rolls, split and toasted -6
- Romaine leaves
- dried oregano -1 tsp.- 4g
- lean ground beef (90% lean) -1 pound - 450 g
- red onion, chopped -1 small
- tomato sauce —1 can (15 ounces) 425 g
- crumbled feta cheese -1/2 cup — 75 g

Preparation

1. Cook the meat, onion, and garlic in a large skillet over medium heat for 6 to 8 minutes, or until the steak is no longer pink. Drain after breaking up the pieces. bring to a boil the tomato sauce, oregano, and stirring. Reduce the heat, cover the pan, and simmer the sauce for 8 to 10 minutes once it has significantly thickened.
2. Fill the bottoms of the rolls with romaine and the meat mixture. Apply fresh tops and sprinkle feta cheese on top.

Nutrition Information

Calories 365, Fat 10 g , Total Carbohydrate 36g, Total Sugars 5.1g , Protein 31.5g, Potassium 635 mg, Sodium 871 mg

Storage:a sealed container is used to store Greek Sloppy Joes for up to 3 -4 days

Reheat: just defrost at room temperature for a few hours

13.2 Beef Barley Skillet

Preparation: 20 minutes
Cooking time 10 minutes
Servings: 4

Ingredients

- Worcestershire sauce -1 tsp. — 4 ml
- quick-cooking barley -3/4 cup -117 g
- chili sauce -1/2 cup — 30 ml
- lean ground beef (90% lean) -1 pound — 450 g
- celery -1/4 cup — 25 g
- Pepper -1/8 tsp.
- diced tomatoes, undrained -1 can (14-1/2 ounces) — 425 ml
- dried marjoram -1/2 tsp.-2 g
- onion, chopped -1 small
- parsley, optional
- green pepper -1/4 cup — 38 g
- Water -1-1/2 cups — 360 ml

Preparation

1. In a medium-hot pan, After sautéing the beef, onion, celery, and green pepper for 5 to 7 minutes, or until the veggies are cooked and the steak is no longer pink, crumble the steak, and then drain. Stir in the next seven ingredients. Drop the heat; it's about to boil over. Barley should be simmered uncovered for 5 to 10 minutes, or until it is tender. If desired, add some chopped parsley.

Nutrition Information

Calories 309, Fat 7.9 g, Total Carbohydrate 21.4g, Total Sugars 4.5g, Protein 37.8g, Potassium 854 mg, Sodium 864 mg

Storage: a sealed container is used to store Beef Barley Skillet for up to 3 -4 days

Reheat: just defrost at room temperature for a few hours

13.3 Brown Rice Stuffed Peppers

Preparation: 20 minutes

Cooking time 15 minutes

Servings: 6

Ingredients

- tomato sauce -1 can (8 ounces) -226 g
- green peppers -6 medium
- uncooked brown rice -3/4 cup – 142 g
- dried oregano-1/4 tsp .- 1 g
- onion, chopped -1 medium
- dried basil -1/4 tsp .- 1 g
- lean ground beef (90% lean) -1 pound- 450 g
- dried thyme-1/4 tsp .- 1 g
- salt -1/2 tsp.-2 g
- Pepper to taste

Preparation

1. Remove the peppers' tops and seeds. In a stockpot, bring 10 cups of water to a boil before adding the peppers and cooking for 5 minutes. Drain and take away. Rice should be made according to the package's instructions.

2. Preheat the oven to 375°F (190°C). In a sizable skillet over medium heat, cook the beef and onion until the meat is no longer pink, shred the meat, and then drain. After incorporating the tomato sauce, herbs, salt, and pepper, cook for 5 minutes without the lid. Add rice by stirring. Eliminate the heat. Rice mixture stuffed into peppers. Place in a small, ungreased baking or casserole dish. Until they are soft, bake the peppers uncovered for 15-20 minutes.

Nutrition Information

Calories 267, Fat 5.7 g, Total Carbohydrate 27.4g, Total Sugars 5.2g, Protein 26.4g, Potassium 730 mg, Sodium 446 mg

Storage: a sealed container is used to store Brown Rice Stuffed Peppers for up to 3 -4 days

Reheat: just defrost at room temperature for a few hours

13.4 Juicy & Delicious Mixed Spice-Burgers

Preparation: 10 minutes

Cooking time 20 minutes

Servings: 6

Ingredients

- ground allspice-3/4 tsp.- 3 g
- 1 garlic clove, minced
- minced fresh mint -2 tbsp.- 6 g
- ground nutmeg -1/4 tsp.- 1 g
- Salt -1/2 tsp.- 2 g
- lean ground beef (90% lean) -1-1/2 pounds – 680 g
- minced fresh parsley -3 tbsp.-9 g
- Optional: Lettuce leaves and refrigerated tzatziki sauce, optional
- Pepper -3/4 tsp.- 3 g
- ground cinnamon-1/2 tsp.- 2 g
- onion, finely chopped -1 medium

Preparation

1. Combine the first nine ingredients. Just enough stirring will mix in the meat

after adding it. Shape into six 4x2 in. oblong patties.

2. Grill or broil patties for 4-6 minutes each side, covered, over medium heat or until an instant-read thermometer reads 160°F (71°C). Serve on a plate with sauce and, if you'd like, place on lettuce leaves.

Nutrition Information
Calories 152, Fat 4.8 g, Total Carbohydrate 2.7g, Total Sugars 0.8g , Protein 23.3g, Potassium 359 mg, Sodium 246 mg
Storage: a sealed container is used to store Juicy & Delicious Mixed Spice-Burgers for up to 3 -4 days
Reheat: just defrost at room temperature for a few hours

13.5 Zucchini Lasagna

Preparation: 20 minutes
Cooking time 40 minutes
Servings: 6
Ingredients
- 2% cottage cheese -1 cup – 226 g
- tomato sauce -1 can (15 ounces) – 425 g
- chopped onion -1/4 cup -28 g
- dried oregano -1/2 tsp. – 2 g
- shredded part-skim mozzarella cheese - 1 cup – 30 g
- dried basil-1/2 tsp. – 2 g
- lean ground beef (90% lean) -1 pound – 450 g
- salt -1/4 tsp.- 1 g
- egg, lightly beaten -1 large
- pepper-1/4 tsp.- 1 g
- Additional shredded mozzarella cheese, optional
- all-purpose flour-3 tbsp.-45 g
- Zucchini -4 medium

Preparation
1. Oven temperature: 375°F (190°C). Cook and crumble beef with onion in a large skillet over medium-high heat for 5–7 minutes, or until the meat is no longer pink. Add the seasonings and tomato sauce and stir. Cook uncovered for 5 minutes after bringing to a boil. Cottage cheese and egg should be combined in a bowl.
2. Slice the zucchini lengthwise into 1/4-inch-thick slices after trimming the ends. Combine the flour and zucchini. Put half of the pieces in a buttered 13 x 9-inch baking dish. Half the beef sauce should be covered with the cottage cheese mixture. Add the remaining zucchini slices and any leftover flour. 1 cup of mozzarella cheese should be added before adding the remaining beef sauce.
3. Bake the dish uncovered for about 40 minutes, or until heated all the way through. If desired, top with additional cheese. Before serving, ten minutes should have passed.

Nutrition Information
Calories 247, Fat 7.5 g, Total Carbohydrate 11.8g, Total Sugars 4.4g, Protein 33.1g, Potassium 844 mg, Sodium 567 mg
Storage: a sealed container is used to store Zucchini Lasagna for up to 3 -4 days
Reheat: just defrost at room temperature for a few hours

13.6 Korean Beef and Rice

Preparation: 10 minutes
Cooking time 15 minutes
Servings: 4
Ingredients
- green onions, thinly sliced -3
- ground ginger -1/4 tsp.-1g
- crushed red pepper flakes-1/4 tsp.-1g
- reduced-sodium soy sauce -1/4 cup -65 ml
- packed brown sugar -1/4 cup -36 g
- hot cooked brown rice -2 cups – 292 g
- lean ground beef (90% lean) -1 pound – 450 g

- pepper-1/4 tsp.-1g
- sesame oil -2 tsp.-8 ml
- garlic cloves, minced -3

Preparation

1. Cook the beef and garlic in a large skillet over medium heat for 6 to 8 minutes, or until the steak is no longer pink. As the beef cooks, crumble it. While you wait, combine the ingredients in a small bowl with the oil, soy sauce, and brown sugar.
2. Well-heated pork with sauce. Include with the rice. On top, sprinkle some green onions.

Nutrition Information
Calories 357, Fat 9.9 g, Total Carbohydrate 28g, Total Sugars 9.4g , Protein 37.1g, Potassium 593 mg, Sodium 611 mg
Storage:a sealed container is used to store Korean Beef and Rice for up to 3 -4 days
Reheat: just defrost at room temperature for a few hours

13.7 California Burger Wraps

Preparation: 10 minutes
Cooking time 20 minutes
Servings: 4
Ingredients

- Chopped cherry tomatoes, optional
- salt -1/2 tsp.- 2 g
- crumbled feta cheese -1/3 cup – 50 g
- Bibb lettuce leaves -8
- pepper -1/4 tsp.- 1 g
- ripe avocado, peeled and cut into 8 slices -1/2 medium
- Miracle Whip Light -2 tbsp.-30 g
- chopped red onion -1/4 cup -40 g
- lean ground beef (90% lean) -1 pound – 450 g

Preparation

1. Thoroughly combine the beef, salt, and pepper in a large dish. Make eight patties that are 1/2 inch thick.

2. Grill or broil hamburgers for 3–4 minutes on each side, covered, over medium heat, or until an instant-read thermometer registers 160° F (71°C). Lettuce leaves should be stuffed with hamburgers. Spread a feta and Miracle Whip concoction over the hamburgers. Add tomatoes, red onion, and avocado as desired.

Nutrition Information
Calories 334, Fat 17.2 g, Total Carbohydrate 6.7g, Total Sugars 2.3g, Protein 37.1g, Potassium 686 mg, Sodium 561 mg
Storage:a sealed container is used to store California Burger Wraps for up to 3 -4 days
Reheat: just defrost at room temperature for a few hours

13.8 Spanish Rice

Preparation: 10 minutes
Cooking time 10 minutes
Servings: 4
Ingredients

- lean ground beef (90% lean) -1 pound – 450 g
- chili powder -1 tsp.- 4g
- tomato sauce -1 can (15 ounces) – 425 g
- garlic powder -1/2 tsp.- 2g
- green pepper, chopped -1 medium
- no-salt-added diced tomatoes, drained - 1 can (14-1/2 ounces) -411g
- Chopped green onions, optional
- ground cumin -1 tsp.- 4g
- salt -1/4 tsp.- 1 g
- cooked brown rice -2-2/3 cups – 500 g
- onion, chopped -1 large

Preparation

1. Cook the beef, onion, and pepper in a large skillet over medium heat for 6 to 8 minutes, or until the steak is no longer pink and the onion is soft. Drain.

2. Seasonings, tomato sauce, and other components are included before boiling. Rice needs to be thoroughly heated while occasionally being stirred. If you'd like, garnish with green onions.

Nutrition Information

Calories 627, Fat 10.4 g, Total Carbohydrate 88.2g, Total Sugars 9.9g, Protein 44.8g, Potassium 1458 mg, Sodium 798mg

Storage: a sealed container is used to store Spanish Rice for up to 3 -4 days

Reheat: just defrost at room temperature for a few hours

13.9 Skillet Beef Tamales

Preparation: 10 minutes

Cooking time 20 minutes

Servings: 5

Ingredients

- lean ground beef (90% lean) -1 pound – 450 g
- chopped sweet red pepper -1/3 cup – 45 g
- salsa -2 cups – 260 g
- water -2 tbsp.-30 ml
- frozen corn -3/4 cup – 60 g
- shredded reduced-fat cheddar cheese - 3/4 cup – 84 g
- chopped green pepper -1/3 cup – 45 g
- corn tortillas (6 inches), halved and cut into 1/2-inch strips -6
- fat-free sour cream -5 tbsp.-75 g

Preparation

1. In a large skillet, saute the beef and peppers in cooking spray over medium heat for 6 to 8 minutes, or until the steak is no longer pink and the vegetables are mushy. Drain after shredding the beef. Water, corn, and salsa have all been included. boiling point.
2. Add the tortilla strips and stir. For 10-15 minutes, cook the tortillas on a lower heat under a cover. When

covered, the cheese should melt after a further 2 to 3 minutes of simmering. It is advised to use sour cream.

Nutrition Information

Calories 366, Fat 12.6 g, Total Carbohydrate 27.3g, Total Sugars 5.8g, Protein 36.4g, Potassium 833 mg, Sodium 818 mg

Storage: a sealed container is used to store Skillet Beef Tamales for up to 3 -4 days

Reheat: just defrost at room temperature for a few hours

13.10 Beef & Bulgur-Stuffed Zucchini Boats

Preparation: 30 minutes

Cooking time 30 minutes

Servings: 4

Ingredients

- tomato sauce -1-1/2 cups – 367 g
- onion, finely chopped -1 large
- pepper -1/4 tsp.- 1 g
- salsa -1/2 cup -65 g
- lean ground beef (90% lean) -1 pound - 450 g
- bulgur -1/2 cup -70 g
- shredded reduced-fat cheddar cheese - 1/2 cup – 56 g
- sweet red pepper, chopped -1 small
- Zucchini -4 medium

Preparation

1. Adjust the oven to 350°F (176°C). Each zucchini should be cut in half lengthwise. Slice the flesh, keeping the shell (about 1/4 inch).
2. Cook the beef, onion, and red pepper in a large skillet over medium heat for 6 to 8 minutes, or until the meat is no longer pink. Drain. Add the bulgur, pepper, tomato sauce, and zucchini meat. boiling level Cooking time for bulgur should be between 12 and 15 minutes with a cover on. Mix in salsa. Fill the zucchini shells with a spoonful.

3. Put in a 13 x 9-inch baking dish that has been sprayed with cooking spray. 20 minutes of covered baking. On top, sprinkle some shredded cheese. Bake the filling for a further 10-15 minutes uncovered, or until the zucchini is soft.

Nutrition Information

Calories 407, Fat 12.6 g, Total Carbohydrate 31.2g, Total Sugars 10.2g, Protein 44.5g, Potassium 1468 mg, Sodium 703 mg

Storage:a sealed container is used to store Beef & Bulgur-Stuffed Zucchini Boats for up to 3 -4 days

Reheat: just defrost at room temperature for a few hours

14 SNACKS & APPETIZERS

14.1 Horseradish Deviled Eggs

Preparation: 10 minutes
Cooking time 20 minutes
Servings: 12

Ingredients

- Dash pepper
- ground mustard -1/4 tsp.-1 g
- salt -1/8 tsp.
- dill weed -1/2 tsp.-2 g
- Hard-boiled large eggs -6
- prepared horseradish -1 to 2 tbsp.-15 g
- Dash paprika
- Mayonnaise -1/4 cup -58 g

Preparation

1. Eggs should be split lengthwise. Remove yolks, and reserve whites. Mash the yolks in a basin. Mix well before adding the mayonnaise, horseradish, dill, mustard, salt, and pepper. Egg whites can be piped or spooned in. Add paprika to the mixture. Keep chilled until serving.

Nutrition Information

Calories 56, Fat 4.1 g , Total Carbohydrate 1.6g, Total Sugars 0.7g , Protein 3.2g, Potassium 40 mg, Sodium 98 mg

Storage:a sealed container is used to store Horseradish Deviled Eggs for up to 3 -4 days

Reheat: just defrost at room temperature for a few hours

14.2 Chia Seed Protein Bites

Preparation: 10 minutes
Cooking time 00 minutes
Servings: 18

Ingredients

- vanilla or chocolate protein powder - 1/4 cup – 30 g
- chia seeds -1/2 cup – 86 g
- Additional unsweetened shredded coconut, optional
- almond butter -1/2 cup -128 g
- unsweetened shredded coconut -1/4 cup – 20 g
- quick-cooking oats -1-1/2 cups -120 g
- honey -1/2 cup -170 g

Preparation

1. Combine the first 6 ingredients in a big bowl. Refrigerate for one hour or until rollable. Form into 1-1/2" balls. Adding more coconut is optional. Place in the fridge to store.

Nutrition Information

Calories 366, Fat 12.6 g, Total Carbohydrate 27.3g, Total Sugars 5.8g, Protein 36.4g, Potassium 833 mg, Sodium 818 mg

Storage:a sealed container is used to store Skillet Beef Tamales for up to 3 -4 days

Reheat: just defrost at room temperature for a few hours

14.3 Kale Chips

Preparation: 10 minutes
Cooking time 15 minutes
Servings: 4

Ingredients

- kale, leaves torn into pieces - 16 cups – 1.7 Kg
- salt -¼ tsp.- 1 g
- extra-virgin olive oil -1 tbsp.-15 ml

Preparation

1. Oven rack positions: upper third and centre; temperature: 400 degrees F (204 C).
2. If the kale is moist, dry it off completely with a clean kitchen towel before transferring it to a large dish. Add salt and oil to the greens before serving. The kale leaves should be evenly coated by massaging salt and oil onto them with your hands. Make sure the kale leaves don't overlap as you place it on 2 large rimmed baking sheets. (If there isn't enough room for all the kale, make the chips in batches.)
3. Bake for 8 to 12 minutes, turning the pans about halfway through to bake until the majority of the leaves are crisp. (If baking a batch on a single baking sheet, check after 8 minutes to avoid scorching.)

Nutrition Information

Calories 162, Fat 3.5 g, Total Carbohydrate 28g, Total Sugars 0g, Protein 8g, Potassium 1316 , Sodium 263 mg

Storage: a sealed container is used to store Kale Chips for up to 3 -4 days

Reheat: just defrost at room temperature for a few hours

14.4 Spicy Pumpkin Seeds

Preparation: 10 minutes
Cooking time 45 minutes
Servings: 2 cups

Ingredients

- cayenne pepper 1/4 tsp.- 1 g
- canola oil -2 tbsp.-30 ml
- hot pepper sauce -1/8 to 1/4 tsp.- 1 ml
- salt -1/2 tsp.- 2 g
- fresh pumpkin seeds -2 cups – 276 g
- paprika-1/2 tsp.- 2 g
- ground cumin-1/4 tsp.- 1 g
- Worcestershire sauce -1 tsp.-4 ,l

Preparation

1. Combine the oil, spicy sauce, Worcestershire sauce, and pumpkin seeds in a small bowl. Before coating, the seeds should be seasoned with salt, paprika, cumin, and cayenne.
2. Line the bottom of a 15x10x1-inch baking pan with foil that has been gently oiled. The pumpkin seeds should be dispersed in a pan. Bake until dry and lightly browned for 45 to 50 minutes at 250 degrees, stirring frequently. total cooling When storing, use an airtight container.

Nutrition Information

Calories 219, Fat 19.4 g, Total Carbohydrate 6.4g, Total Sugars 0.5g, Protein 8.5g, Potassium 284 mg, Sodium 161 mg

Storage: a sealed container is used to store Spicy Pumpkin Seeds for up to 3 -4 days

Reheat: just defrost at room temperature for a few hours

14.5 Cinnamon Popcorn

Preparation: 10 minutes
Cooking time 15 minutes
Servings: 4

Ingredients

- ground cinnamon -½ tsp.-2 g
- sugar -2 tsp.-8g
- Butter-flavor nonstick cooking spray
- popped popcorn -8 cups - 192 g

Preparation

1. Oven should be preheated to 350 degrees Fahrenheit (176 C). You can use foil to line a shallow roasting pan. Spread the popcorn in the shallow roasting pan. In a little bowl, mix the cinnamon and sugar. When coating popcorn, cooking spray should be used sparingly and uniformly. To evenly coat, add the cinnamon mixture and toss one more. About 5 minutes of baking will make the crispiest results.

Nutrition Information

Calories 70, Fat 0.7 g , Total Carbohydrate 14.7g, Total Sugars 2.2g, Protein 2.1g, Potassium 54 mg, Sodium 1 mg

Storage:a sealed container is used to store Cinnamon Popcorn for up to 3 -4 days

Reheat: just defrost at room temperature for a few hours

14.6 Chile-Lime Peanuts

Preparation: 10 minutes
Cooking time 50 minutes
Servings: 48

Ingredients

- lime juice -6 tbsp.- 90 ml
- kosher salt -4 tsp.-16g
- unsalted cocktail peanuts -6 cups -880 g
- cayenne pepper -1/2-1 tsp.-4 g
- chili powder6 tbsp.- 45 g

Preparation

1. Position the oven racks and set the temperature to 250 degrees F. (121 C).
2. Combine lime juice, cayenne, chilli powder, salt, and salt in a large bowl. Add the peanuts and thoroughly coat. On two sizable rimmed baking pans, spread evenly. Divide.
3. Bake the mixture until dry for about 45 minutes, stirring every 15 minutes. Permit to completely cool. For storage, use an airtight container.

Nutrition Information

Calories 108, Fat 9.2 g, Total Carbohydrate 3.9g, Total Sugars 0.8g , Protein 4.9g, Potassium 153 mg, Sodium 207 mg

Storage:a sealed container is used to store Chile-Lime Peanuts for up to 3 -4 days

Reheat: just defrost at room temperature for a few hours

14.7 Shrimp Cocktail

Preparation: 10 minutes
Cooking time 00 minutes
Servings: 6

Ingredients

- Tomato -1 medium
- minced fresh cilantro -2 tbsp.-12 g
- green chiles -1 can (4 ounces) -113 g
- Italian salad dressing -1/2 cup -117 g
- hot pepper sauce -1/8 tsp.
- Shrimp -1 pound – 450 g
- Romaine leaves
- honey -2 tsp.-8 g
- green onions -3

Preparation

1. Combine the first eight ingredients in a sizable bowl. Place covered in the refrigerator for at least one hour.
2. You should line 6 cocktail glasses or serving utensils with romaine lettuce. Using a slotted spoon, put about 1/2 cup of the shrimp mixture into each.

Nutrition Information

Calories 131, Fat 6.3 g, Total Carbohydrate 5.7g, Total Sugars 4.4g , Protein 10.9g, Potassium 83 mg, Sodium 180 mg

Storage:a sealed container is used to store Shrimp Cocktail for up to 3 -4 days

Reheat: just defrost at room temperature for a few hours

14.8 Curried Cashews

Preparation: 10 minutes
Cooking time 40 minutes
Servings: 48

Ingredients

- unsalted cashews -6 cups -822 g
- lemon juice -6 tbsp. – 90 ml
- kosher salt -4 tsp.-16 g
- curry powder -6 tbsp. – 38 g

Preparation

1. Oven rack placement and temperature adjustment to 250 degrees F (121 C).
2. Combine salt, lemon juice, and curry powder in a large bowl. It is necessary to coat and add cashews. On two sizable rimmed baking pans, spread evenly. Divide.
3. Bake the mixture until dry for about 45 minutes, stirring every 15 minutes. Permit to completely cool. For storage, use an airtight container.

Nutrition Information

Calories 101, Fat 8.1 g, Total Carbohydrate 6.1g, Total Sugars 0.9g , Protein 2.7g, Potassium 111 mg, Sodium 197 mg

Storage: a sealed container is used to store Curried Cashews for up to 3 -4 days

Reheat: just defrost at room temperature for a few hours

Greek Yogurt with Fruit & Nuts

Preparation: 05 minutes

Cooking time 00 minutes

Servings:1

Ingredients

- chopped walnuts -1 ½ tsp.-6 g
- plain non-fat Greek yogurt -⅓ cup -50 g
- dried apricots -3

Preparation

1. In a bowl, put the yoghurt. Apricots and walnuts are added after stirring.

Nutrition Information

Calories 257, Fat 18.6 g, Total Carbohydrate 17.3g, Total Sugars 12.8g, Protein 10.4g, Potassium 325 mg, Sodium 18 mg

Storage: a sealed container is used to store Greek Yogurt with Fruit & Nuts for up to 3 -4 days

Reheat: just defrost at room temperature for a few hours

14.9 Apricot-Ginger Energy Balls

Preparation: 10 minutes

Cooking time 00 minutes

Servings: 32

Ingredients

- tahini -6 tbsp.-90 g
- Pinch of salt
- rolled oats -¾ cup – 60 g
- dried apricots -1 ½ cups – 60 g
- ground ginger -¾ tsp.- 3 g
- honey -3 tbsp.-45 g
- unsweetened coconut -¾ cup -60 g

Preparation

1. In a food processor, combine the following ingredients: apricots, oats, coconut, honey, ginger, and salt. The ingredients should be finely chopped after 10 to 20 pulses of processing until the mixture is crumbly but still forms a cohesive ball when pressed. After that, process for another minute or so, scraping the sides as required.
2. Squeeze around 1 tablespoon of the mixture between your hands to form a ball. Wet your hands to avoid the mixture from sticking to them. Place in a box for storage. Repeat with the remaining mixture.

Nutrition Information

Calories 40, Fat 2.3 g , Total Carbohydrate 4.6g, Total Sugars 2.5g , Protein 0.9g, Potassium 27 mg, Sodium 8 mg

Storage: a sealed container is used to store Skillet Beef Tamales for up to 3 -4 days

Reheat: just defrost at room temperature for a few hours

15 SMOOTHIES

15.1 Strawberry Tofu Smoothie

Preparation: 10 minutes

Cooking time 00 minutes

Servings: 2

Ingredients

- almond butter -2 tbsp.- 30 g
- liquid Stevia (adjust to taste) -3-5 drops
- vanilla extract -1 tsp. 4 ml
- lemon juice -1 tsp. 4 ml
- ½ cup ice cubes
- Tofu -12 oz.- 340 g
- almond milk -1 cup – 240 ml
- strawberries (chopped) -1 cup -166 g

Preparation

1. The ingredients should all be combined in the blender, with the exception of the ice cubes. Blend everything up until it's smooth.
2. The additional ingredients and the ice cubes should be thoroughly blended in the blender.
3. Add any desired toppings and serve right away.

Nutrition Information

Calories 523, Fat 44.9 g, Total Carbohydrate 18.4g, Total Sugars 9.6g, Protein 20.9g, Potassium 804 mg, Sodium 43 mg

Storage:a sealed container is used to store Strawberry Tofu Smoothie for up to 3 -4 days

Reheat: just defrost at room temperature for a few hours

15.2 Avocado Smoothie with Leafy Greens

Preparation: 10 minutes

Cooking time 00 minutes

Servings: 2

Ingredients

- ice cubes -½ cup
- Water -2 cups – 480 ml
- baby kale -1 cup – 85 g
- mint sprigs -2
- lemon juice -1 tbsp.
- baby spinach -2 cups – 60 g
- avocado -1

Preparation

1. In a powerful blender, combine the spinach, kale, mint, avocado, lemon juice, and water. Lastly, add the ice cubes.
2. Blend the ingredients at high speed until it is smooth.
3. You can add a few drops of Stevia to the smoothie if you want it to be sweeter.

Nutrition Information

Calories 230, Fat 20 g , Total Carbohydrate 13.1g, Total Sugars 0.8g, Protein 4g, Potassium 719 mg, Sodium 51 mg

Storage:a sealed container is used to store Avocado Smoothie with Leafy Greens for up to 3 -4 days

Reheat: just defrost at room temperature for a few hours

15.3 Green Smoothie

Preparation: 10 minutes

Cooking time 00 minutes

Servings: 2

Ingredients

- frozen avocado -½ cup – 100g
- spinach -2 cups – 60 g
- almond butter -1 tbsp.-15 g
- protein powder -¼ cup – 8.4 g
- vanilla extract -1 tsp.-4 g
- almond milk (unsweetened) -1 cup – 240 ml
- A few drops Stevia sweetener
- 1 cup ice cubes

Preparation

1. In a powerful blender, combine the spinach, kale, mint, avocado, lemon juice, and water. Lastly, add the ice cubes.
2. Blend the ingredients at high speed until it is smooth.
3. You can add a few drops of Stevia to the smoothie if you want it to be sweeter.

Nutrition Information

Calories 424, Fat 40.9 g, Total Carbohydrate 13g, Total Sugars 4.8g, Protein 8.8g, Potassium 751 mg, Sodium 55 mg

Storage: a sealed container is used to store Green Smoothie for up to 3 -4 days

Reheat: just defrost at room temperature for a few hours

15.4 Strawberry-Pineapple Smoothie

Preparation: 10 minutes

Cooking time 00 minutes

Servings: 1

Ingredients

- almond butter -1 tbsp. – 15 g
- chilled unsweetened almond milk,- ¾ cup – 75 ml
- strawberries -1 cup -150 g
- chopped fresh pineapple -1 cup – 165 g

Preparation

1. In a blender, combine strawberries, pineapple, almond milk, and almond butter. Process until smooth, adjusting the consistency with additional almond milk as necessary. Serve right away.

Nutrition Information

Calories 240, Fat 10 g, Total Carbohydrate 37.7g, Total Sugars 25g, Protein 4.6g, Potassium 300 mg, Sodium 3 mg

Storage: a sealed container is used to store Strawberry-Pineapple Smoothie for up to 3 -4 days

Reheat: just defrost at room temperature for a few hours

15.5 Watermelon Smoothie

Preparation: 10 minutes

Cooking time 00 minutes

Servings: 4

Ingredients

- watermelon (cubed and chilled) -2 cups -308 g
- 1 lime (juiced)
- fresh mint leaves (to taste) -5-10
- soy milk -½ cup -120 ml
- stevia liquid -5 drops
- 3 cups ice

Preparation

1. Blend all the ingredients together in a blender until thoroughly combined.
2. Dish out and find joy

Nutrition Information

Calories 46, Fat 0.7 g , Total Carbohydrate 9.6g, Total Sugars 6.2g , Protein 1.7g, Potassium 153 mg, Sodium 23 mg

Storage: a sealed container is used to store Watermelon Smoothie for up to 3 -4 days

Reheat: just defrost at room temperature for a few hours

15.6 Carrot Smoothie

Preparation: 10 minutes

Cooking time 00 minutes

Servings: 3

Ingredients

- finely shredded orange peel -½ tsp- 2 g
- ice cubes -1 ½ cups
- orange juice -1 cup – 240 ml
- Orange peel curls -3 (1 inch) pieces
- Carrots -1 cup - 120 g

Preparation

1. Blend all the ingredients together in a blender until thoroughly combined.
2. Dish out and find joy

Nutrition Information

Calories 53, Fat 0.2 g , Total Carbohydrate 12.3g, Total Sugars 8.7g, Protein 0.9g, Potassium 283 mg, Sodium 26 mg

Storage:a sealed container is used to store Carrot Smoothie for up to 3 -4 days

Reheat: just defrost at room temperature for a few hours

15.7 Blueberry Smoothie

Preparation: 05 minutes

Cooking time 00 minutes

Servings: 2

Ingredients

- vanilla extract -1/2 tsp.- 2 g
- unsweetened coconut milk -14 oz. canned -400 ml
- blueberries (fresh or frozen) -1/2 cup – 72 g
- unsweetened almond milk -1/2 cup - 120 ml
- pea protein powder -4 tbsp.-60 g

Preparation

1. Blend all the ingredients together in a blender until thoroughly combined.
2. Dish out and find joy

Nutrition Information

Calories 610, Fat 50.3 g, Total Carbohydrate 17.9g , Total Sugars 10.5g, Protein 29.1g, Potassium 599 mg, Sodium 405 mg

Storage: a sealed container is used to store Blueberry Smoothie for up to 3 -4 days

Reheat: just defrost at room temperature for a few hours

15.8 Chocolate Avocado Smoothie

Preparation: 10 minutes

Cooking time 00 minutes

Servings: 2

Ingredients

- liquid Stevia -6-7 drops
- water -1/2 cup – 120 ml
- full-fat coconut milk -1 cup – 240 ml
- ripe avocado -1/2
- lime juice -1 tsp. – 4 g
- Fresh mint (for decoration)
- cocoa powder -3 tbsp.-45 g
- pinch mineral salt

Preparation

1. 1 Blend all the ingredients together in a blender until thoroughly combined
2. Dish out and find joy

Nutrition Information

Calories 139, Fat 11 g , Total Carbohydrate 13g, Total Sugars 0.8g, Protein 3.3g, Potassium 499 mg, Sodium 9 mg

Storage:a sealed container is used to store Chocolate Avocado Smoothie for up to 3 -4 days

Reheat: just defrost at room temperature for a few hours

15.9 Chocolate Shake

Preparation: 10 minutes

Cooking time 00 minutes

Servings: 2

Ingredients

- full fat coconut milk-1.5 cup – 420 ml
- vanilla extract -1/2 tsp.-2 g
- almond butter -2 tbsp.-30 g
- monk fruit sweetener -1.5 tbsp.-3 g
- cocoa powder2 tbsp.-30 g

Preparation

1. Blend all the ingredients together in a blender until thoroughly combined
2. Dish out and find joy

Nutrition Information

Calories 527, Fat 52.3 g, Total Carbohydrate 17.6g, Total Sugars 6.9g, Protein 8.5g, Potassium 730 mg, Sodium 29 mg

Storage:a sealed container is used to store Chocolate Shake for up to 3 -4 days

Reheat: just defrost at room temperature for a few hours

15.10 Pumpkin Spice Smoothie

Preparation: 10 minutes

Cooking time 00 minutes

Servings: 1

Ingredients

- Chocolate Collagen Powder -1 scoop
- 2 ice cubes
- almond butter -2 tbsp.-30 g
- unsweetened almond milk -8 oz.-225 ml
- pinch of pumpkin pie spice

Preparation

1. Blend all the ingredients together in a blender until thoroughly combined
2. Dish out and find joy

Nutrition Information

Calories 261, Fat 21.3 g, Total Carbohydrate 8g, Total Sugars 1.4g , Protein 14.7g, Potassium 419 mg, Sodium 225 mg

Storage: a sealed container is used to store Pumpkin Spice Smoothie for up to 3 -4 days

Reheat: just defrost at room temperature for a few hours

16 DRINKS

16.1 Spiced Apple Tea

Preparation: 10 minutes

Cooking time 00 minutes

Servings: 4

Ingredients

- unsweetened apple juice -2 cups – 480 ml
- whole cloves -6
- water -3 cups – 720 ml
- cinnamon herbal tea -3 bags
- cinnamon stick - 1

Preparation

1. Combine the juice, the cinnamon stick, and the cloves in a medium saucepan. Bring to a boil by using high heat. On low heat, simmer for ten minutes. Another medium saucepan is now receiving water. Bring to a boil by using high heat. After adding the tea bags, the pot should be turned off the heat. Remove and throw away the tea bags.
2. The mixture should be filtered, and the spices should be discarded. Juice and tea should be blended. Serve warm, if desired, with additional cinnamon sticks, or cool and serve with chilled ice. (Tea can be heated and made in advance.)

Nutrition Information

Calories 70, Fat 0.8 g, Total Carbohydrate 16.9 g, Total Sugars 13.6g, Protein 0.3g, Potassium 187 mg, Sodium 17 mg

Storage: a sealed container is used to store Spiced Apple Tea for up to 3 -4 days

Reheat: just defrost at room temperature for a few hours

16.2 Spiced Citrus Tea

Preparation: 10 minutes

Cooking time 00 minutes

Servings: 1

Ingredients

- Honey (optional)
- Citrus Tea bag -1 Spiced
- Orange slices (optional)
- orange juice -1 to 2 teaspoons – 8 ml
- Boiling water

Preparation

1. Put a tea bag in the glass or mug. 3 to 5 minutes with a tea bag in boiling water. Squeeze the liquid out of the tea bag after removing it. Delete the tea bag. If desired, serve with orange juice and honey. Orange slices are a nice garnish.

Nutrition Information

Calories 71, Fat 0 g, Total Carbohydrate 19.1g, Total Sugars 18.0g, Protein 0.2g, Potassium 53 mg, Sodium 8 mg

Storage: a sealed container is used to store Spiced Citrus Tea for up to 3 -4 days

Reheat: just defrost at room temperature for a few hours

16.3 Ocean Water

Preparation: 10 minutes

Cooking time 00 minutes

Servings: 1

Ingredients

- blue food coloring -2 drops
- white grape juice, chilled -1/2 cup (4 ounces) -113 ml
- club soda, chilled -1/4 cup (2 ounces) – 56 ml

Preparation

1. Food colouring should be added to white grape juice, which should then be thoroughly mixed with a spoon. Club soda should be added and mixed three to four times. Take a drink now.

Nutrition Information

Calories 71, Fat 0 g, Total Carbohydrate 19.1g, Total Sugars 18.7g , Protein 0.2g, Potassium 53 mg, Sodium 8 mg

Storage: a sealed container is used to store Ocean Water for up to 3 -4 days

Reheat: just defrost at room temperature for a few hours

16.4 Orange Spice Coffee Mix

Preparation: 05 minutes

Cooking time 00 minutes

Servings: 1

Ingredients

- dried orange peel -1/2 cup -
- ground cloves -4 tsp.-16 g
- freshly ground coffee -1/2 pound -
- ground cinnamon-4 tsp.-16 g

Preparation

1. Add all the ingredients to a large zip-top bag and shake to combine. 12 cups of water and 5 level tablespoons should be used (use more or less to suit taste). Prepare coffee as directed by the automated drip coffeemaker.

Nutrition Information

Calories 99, Fat 2 g, Total Carbohydrate 24.6g, Total Sugars 0.4g, Protein 1.9g, Potassium 345 mg, Sodium 27 mg

Storage: a sealed container is used to store Orange Spice Coffee Mix for up to 3 -4 days

Reheat: just defrost at room temperature for a few hours

16.5 Pink Champagne Punch

Preparation: 10 minutes

Cooking time 00 minutes

Servings: 12

Ingredients

- cilled pink champagne -1 bottle (750 ml)
- sugar-free tropical punch -3 cups- 720 ml
- unsweetened pineapple juice -3 cups- 720 ml
- white cranberry juice drink -3 cups- 720 ml

Preparation

1. Combine all the ingredients in a punch bowl or 1-gallon jug. Serve immediately.

Nutrition Information

Calories 79, Fat 0 g, Total Carbohydrate 19.4g, Total Sugars 18.6g , Protein 0g, Potassium 46mg, Sodium 19 mg

Storage: a sealed container is used to store Pink Champagne Punch for up to 3 -4 days

Reheat: just defrost at room temperature for a few hours

17 Desserts no sugar

17.1 Crispy Peanut Butter Balls

Preparation: 15 minutes
Cooking time 45 minutes
Servings:12
Ingredients

- peanut butter -½ cup -125g
- crispy rice cereal -¾ cup – 22 g
- pure maple syrup -1 tsp- 4 g
- dark chocolate chips, melted -½ cup - 85 g

Preparation

1. Use wax paper or parchment to line a baking pan. In a medium bowl, mix cereal, peanut butter, and maple syrup. Make 12 balls out of the mixture, using about 2 tablespoons each ball. Place the baking sheet that has been prepared. The balls should be frozen for around 15 minutes or until hard.
2. In melted chocolate, roll the balls. Once the chocolate has set, around 15 minutes, return to the freezer.

Nutrition Information

Calories 98, Fat 6.8 g , Total Carbohydrate 7.9g, Total Sugars 4.4g , Protein 2.8g, Potassium 3mg, Sodium 39 mg
Storage:a sealed container is used to store Crispy Peanut Butter Balls for up to 3 -4 days
Reheat: just defrost at room temperature for a few hours

17.2 Date & Pistachio Bites

Preparation: 10 minutes
Cooking time 00 minutes
Servings: 32
Ingredients

- pitted whole dates -2 cups – 450 g
- ground pepper -¼ tsp.- 1g
- ground fennel seeds -1 tsp.-4 g
- golden raisins -1 cup – 200 g
- raw unsalted shelled pistachios -1 cup – 125 g

Preparation

1. Blend dates, pistachios, raisins, fennel, and pepper in a food processor. Process the food until very finely chopped. Create roughly 32 balls with one tablespoon each.

Nutrition Information

Calories 32, Fat 0.9 g , Total Carbohydrate 6g, Total Sugars 4.4g, Protein 0.6g, Potassium 55 mg, Sodium 11 mg
Storage:a sealed container is used to store Date & Pistachio Bites for up to 3 -4 days
Reheat: just defrost at room temperature for a few hours

17.3 Flourless Banana Chocolate Chip Mini Muffins

Preparation: 20 minutes
Cooking time 50 minutes
Servings: 24
Ingredients

- mini chocolate chips -½ cup – 12 g
- salt -¼ tsp. 1 g
- vanilla extract -1 tsp.- 4 g
- baking soda -¼ tsp. 1 g
- mashed ripe banana -1 cup -225 g
- eggs -2 large
- canola oil -3 tbsp.-45 ml
- baking powder-1 tsp.- 4 g
- rolled oats -1 ½ cups – 60 g

Preparation

1. Prepare the oven to 350°F (176°C). In a 24-cup mini muffin tray, spritz some cooking oil.
2. Pulse the oats in a blender until they are pulverised. You should include salt, baking soda, and baking powder. To blend, pulse once or twice. Add the eggs, banana, brown sugar, oil, and vanilla, and blend until thoroughly

combined. Stir in the chocolate chunks. As instructed, put the muffin tins full.

3. Bake for fifteen to seventeen minutes, or until a toothpick inserted in the centre of the cake emerges clean. After five minutes, flip out onto a wire rack to finish cooling in the pan.

Nutrition Information

Calories 53, Fat 2.5 g, Total Carbohydrate 7g, Total Sugars 3.4g, Protein 1.1g, Potassium 65 mg, Sodium 45 mg

Storage: a sealed container is used to store Flourless Banana Chocolate Chip Mini Muffins for up to 3 -4 days

Reheat: just defrost at room temperature for a few hours

17.4 Peanut Butter-Oat Energy Balls

Preparation: 15 minutes
Cooking time 00 minutes
Servings: 12

Ingredients

- natural peanut butter -¼ cup – 62 g
- rolled oats -½ cup – 40 g
- Chia seeds for garnish
- chopped Medjool dates -¾ cup – 168 g

Preparation

1. In a small dish of boiling water, dates should be soaked for 5 to 10 minutes. Drain.
2. Pulse the soaked dates, oats, and peanut butter in a food processor until very finely ground. Form into 12 balls (a scant tablespoon each). If desired, add chia seeds as a garnish. Place in the fridge for at least 15 minutes and as long as a week.

Nutrition Information

Calories 51, Fat 2.9 g, Total Carbohydrate 4.6g, Total Sugars 1.6g, Protein 2.2g, Potassium 12mg, Sodium 1 mg

Storage: a sealed container is used to store Peanut Butter-Oat Energy Balls for up to 3 -4 days

Reheat: just defrost at room temperature for a few hours

17.5 Banana Energy Bites

Preparation: 10 minutes
Cooking time 00 minutes
Servings: 16

Ingredients

- dried cranberries -½ cup – 27 g
- miniature semisweet chocolate pieces - ¼ cup -42 g
- dry quick-cooking rolled oats -1 cup - 81 g
- roasted and salted pumpkin seeds (pepitas)- ½ cup -17 g
- peanut butter -½ cup -125 g
- Banana -1 overripe

Preparation

1. Using a fork, mash the banana in a medium bowl until it is totally smooth. Add the oats, pumpkin seeds, dried cranberries, chocolate bits, and peanut butter. The ingredients should be combined into 32 balls, with 1 tablespoon being used for each nibble. Chill until ready to serve.

Nutrition Information

Calories 91, Fat 5.3 g, Total Carbohydrate 7.5g, Total Sugars 1.8g, Protein 3.8 g, Potassium 52 mg, Sodium 5 mg

Storage: a sealed container is used to store Banana Energy Bites for up to 3 -4 days

Reheat: just defrost at room temperature for a few hours

17.6 Blueberry-Lemon Energy Balls

Preparation: 10 minutes
Cooking time 00 minutes
Servings: 6

Ingredients

- pure maple syrup -2 tbsp.-30 ml
- pitted dates -½ cup- 90 g
- lemon juice -1 tbsp.-15 ml
- grated lemon zest -1 tsp.-4 g
- dried blueberries -¼ cup – 36 g
- Walnuts -¾ cup- 95 g
- old-fashioned rolled oats -¾ cup- 30 g

Preparation

1. Add the blueberries, dates, and walnuts to a food processor and process until smooth. For 7 to 10 seconds, process. Oats, maple syrup, and lemon juice should be added. Once a thick, smooth paste formed, continue for another 20 to 30 seconds. After transferring the paste to a small bowl, add the lemon zest and combine. With your hands, shape and roll the mixture into 18 tiny balls.

Nutrition Information

Calories 198, Fat 10 g , Total Carbohydrte 24.9g, Total Sugars 14.3g, Protein 5.5g, Potassium 238mg, Sodium 2 mg

Storage:a sealed container is used to store Blueberry-Lemon Energy Balls for up to 3 -4 days

Reheat: just defrost at room temperature for a few hours

17.7 Fruit Energy Balls

Preparation: 15 minutes

Cooking time 00 minutes

Servings: 20

Ingredients

- chopped almonds -1 cup – 95 g
- dried apricots -1 cup -155 g
- unsweetened shredded coconut -⅓ cup – 26 g
- dried figs -1 cup – 199 g

Preparation

1. Almonds, figs, and apricots should all be combined in a food processor and pulsed until finely minced. Make tiny balls out of the mixture, then roll them in coconut.

Nutrition Information

Calories 68, Fat 3.6 g , Total Carbohydrate 8.6g, Total Sugars 5.8g , Protein 1.6g, Potassium 123mg, Sodium 2 mg

Storage:a sealed container is used to store Fruit Energy Balls for up to 3 -4 days

Reheat: just defrost at room temperature for a few hours

17.8 Apricot-Sunflower Granola Bars

Preparation: 10 minutes

Cooking time 00 minutes

Servings: 24

Ingredients

- dried apricots -1 cup – 165 g
- sunflower seed butter -½ cup – 120 g
- rolled oats -3 cups – 240 g
- unsalted pepitas, toasted -½ cup – 47 g
- ground cinnamon -1 tsp-4 g
- crispy brown rice cereal -1 cup – 200 g
- salt -¼ tsp.-1 g
- light corn syrup -⅔ cup – 255 ml
- unsalted sunflower seeds, toasted -½ cup – 47 g

Preparation

1. Warm the oven to 325°F (162°C). The bottom, borders, and sides of a 9 by 13-inch baking pan should be lined with parchment paper. Cooking spray should be lightly applied to the parchment paper.
2. 2. In a sizable bowl, mix the oats, rice cereal, apricots, pepitas, sunflower seeds, and salt.
3. 3. In a microwave-safe bowl, mix the rice syrup (or corn syrup), sunflower butter, and cinnamon. a microwave interval of 30 seconds (or heat in a saucepan over medium heat for 1 minute). To blend the dry ingredients,

stir in the addition. transferring to the prepared pan, and using a spatula, pushing firmly into the pan.

4. 4. For chewier bars, bake for 20 to 25 minutes, or until the rims are just beginning to colour but the centre is still soft. Bake the bars an additional 30 to 35 minutes to achieve crunchier bars, or until the edges are golden brown and the centres are still slightly mushy. At body temperature, both are malleable and become harder as they cool.

5. 5. Lift the baked goods out of the pan and lay them on a chopping board after they have cooled in the pan for 10 minutes (it will still be soft). Allow the bars to chill for an additional 30 minutes without separating after cutting them into 24 bars. Slice the bars after they have cooled.

Nutrition Information

Calories 113, Fat 4.3 g, Total Carbohydrate 17.2g, Total Sugars 6.3g, Protein 3.3g, Potassium 63 mg, Sodium 59 mg

Storage: a sealed container is used to store Apricot-Sunflower Granola Bars for up to 3 -4 days

Reheat: just defrost at room temperature for a few hours

17.9 Date-Pistachio Granola Bars

Preparation: 20 minutes

Cooking time 00 minutes

Servings: 12

Ingredients

- crispy brown rice cereal -1 cup -31 g
- tahini -½ cup -17 g
- salt -¼ teaspoon – 1 g
- old-fashioned rolled oats -3 cups -120 g
- finely chopped pitted dates-1 cup -178 g
- hazelnuts, toasted and chopped -½ cup – 57 g
- ground cardamom -1 tsp. – 4g
- brown rice syrup -⅔ cup – 22g g
- unsalted pistachios, toasted and chopped -½ cup – 50 g

Preparation

1. Turn the oven's temperature up to 325 degrees. The bottom, borders, and sides of a 9 by 13-inch baking pan should be lined with parchment paper. Cooking spray should be lightly applied to the parchment paper.

2. 2. In a big bowl, mix the oats, rice cereal, dates, hazelnuts, pistachios, and salt.

3. 3. Combine the cardamom, tahini, and rice syrup (or corn syrup) in a bowl that can be heated in the microwave. a microwave interval of 30 seconds (or heat in a saucepan over medium heat for 1 minute). To blend the dry ingredients, stir in the addition. transferring to the prepared pan, and using a spatula, pushing firmly into the pan. transferring to the prepared pan, and using a spatula, pushing firmly into the pan.

4. 4. For chewier bars, bake for 20 to 25 minutes, or until the rims are just beginning to colour but the centre is still soft. Bake the bars an additional 30 to 35 minutes to achieve crunchier bars, or until the edges are golden brown and the centres are still slightly mushy. At body temperature, both are malleable and become harder as they cool.

5. 5. Lift the baked goods out of the pan and lay them on a chopping board after they have cooled in the pan for 10 minutes (it will still be soft). Allow the bars to chill for an additional 30 minutes without separating after cutting them into 24 bars. Slice the bars after they have cooled.

Nutrition Information

Calories 131, Fat 4.6 g, Total Carbohydrate 21.8g, Total Sugars 10.5g, Protein 3g, Potassium 123mg, Sodium 37 mg

Storage: a sealed container is used to store Date-Pistachio Granola Bars for up to 3 -4 days
Reheat: just defrost at room temperature for a few hours

17.10 Carrot Cake Energy Bites

Preparation: 10 minutes
Cooking time 00 minutes
Servings: 22

Ingredients

- ground cinnamon -¾ tsp.- 3 g
- carrots , finely chopped -2 medium
- pitted dates -1 cup – 225 g
- ground turmeric -¼ tsp.-1 g
- vanilla extract -1 tsp.-4 g
- chia seeds -¼ cup – 43 g
- Pinch of ground pepper
- ground ginger -½ tsp.- 2g
- salt-¼ tsp.-1 g
- chopped pecans -¼ cup – 30 g
- old-fashioned rolled oats -½ cup – 40 g

Preparation

1. Combine the dates, oats, pecans, and chia seeds in a food processor and pulse several times to chop and blend.
2. Combine the carrots with the other seasonings, including the salt, pepper, vanilla, cinnamon, ginger, and turmeric. Mixture should be processed until it forms a paste.
3. Shape the mixture into balls using a tiny bit of 1 Tbsp each ball.

Nutrition Information
Calories 45, Total Fat 1.1g, Total Carbohydrate 8.9g , Total Sugars 5.5g , Protein 1.1g, Potassium 123mg, Sodium 31mg
Storage: a sealed container is used to store Carrot Cake Energy Bites for up to 3 -4 days
Reheat: just defrost at room temperature for a few hours

18 10 weeks Meal Plan

18.1 Week 1

Day	Breakfast	Lunch	Dinner	Snacks	Dessert
1	Milk with Overnight Oats	Chicken Salad	Creamy Shrimp & Mushroom Pasta	Horseradish Deviled Eggs	Crispy Peanut Butter Balls
2	Apple Muffins	Baked Garlicky Salmon Balls	Asparagus Tofu Stir-Fry	Chia Seed Protein Bites	Blueberry-Lemon Energy Balls
3	Lemon Avocado Toast	Broccoli Soup	Ruby Raspberry Slaw	Kale Chips	Banana Energy Bites
4	Spinach Egg White Muffins	Lemony Parsley Baked Cod	Lemon Chicken & Potatoes with Kale	Spicy Pumpkin Seeds	Peanut Butter-Oat Energy Balls
5	Overnight Light Peanut Butter Oats	Korean Beef and Rice	Skillet Beef Tamales	Chile-Lime Peanuts	Date & Pistachio Bites
6	Milk with Peaches quinoa	Chicken & Asparagus Bake	Easy Caribbean Chicken	Cinnamon Popcorn	Carrot Cake Energy Bites
7	Breakfast Egg Salad	Seasoned Cod	Tofu Scramble	Shrimp Cocktail	Fruit Energy Balls

18.2 Week 2

Day	Breakfast	Lunch	Dinner	Snacks	Dessert
1	Pumpkin Spice Smoothie	Greek Sloppy Joes	Garlicky Shrimp & Broccoli	Spicy Pumpkin Seeds	Fruit Energy Balls
2	Poached Eggs	Beef & Bulgur-Stuffed Zucchini Boats	Red Pepper Chicken	Chia Seed Protein Bites	Apricot-Sunflower Granola Bars
3	Breakfast Cereal	Chicken Tetrazzini	California Burger Wraps	Cinnamon Popcorn	Date-Pistachio Granola Bars
4	Banana Nut Muffins	Cauliflower Chicken Fried "Rice	Lemony Parsley Baked Cod	Shrimp Cocktail	Carrot Cake Energy Bites
5	Lemon Avocado Toast	Chickpea & Potato Curry	Easy Caribbean Chicken	Chile-Lime Peanuts	Blueberry-Lemon Energy Balls
6	Milk with Peaches quinoa	Garlicky Green Beans	Broccoli Tuna Casserole	Kale Chips	Banana Energy Bites
7	Coconut Muffins	Seasoned Cod	Cauliflower Alfredo Sauce	Horseradish Deviled Eggs	Date & Pistachio Bites

18.3 Week 3

Day	Breakfast	Lunch	Dinner	Snacks	Dessert
1	Lemon Avocado Toast	Chicken Salad	Stuffed Potatoes with Salsa & Beans	Chile-Lime Peanuts	Blueberry-Lemon Energy Balls
2	Milk with Peaches quinoa	Asparagus Tofu Stir-Fry	Lentil-Tomato Soup	Kale Chips	Banana Energy Bites
3	Overnight Light Peanut Butter Oats	Tuna Nicoise Salad	Shrimp and Cauliflower Bake	Horseradish Deviled Eggs	Date & Pistachio Bites
4	Multigrain Chia Waffles	Vegetarian Linguine	Creamy Chicken Rice Soup	Spicy Pumpkin Seeds	Fruit Energy Balls
5	Poached Eggs	Marinated Beet Salad	Walnut-Rosemary Crusted Salmon	Chia Seed Protein Bites	Apricot-Sunflower Granola Bars
6	Avocado-Egg Toast	Garlicky Green Beans	Turkey and Vegetable Barley Soup	Cinnamon Popcorn	Date-Pistachio Granola Bars
7	Quinoa Breakfast Cereal	Quinoa Tabbouleh	Red Pepper & Parmesan Tilapia	Shrimp Cocktail	Carrot Cake Energy Bites

18.4 Week 4

Day	Breakfast	Lunch	Dinner	Snacks	Dessert
1	Poached Eggs	Greek Sloppy Joes	Marinated Beet Salad	Shrimp Cocktail	Blueberry-Lemon Energy Balls
2	Avocado-Egg Toast	Beef & Bulgur-Stuffed Zucchini Boats	Garlicky Green Beans	Horseradish Deviled Eggs	Peanut Butter-Oat Energy Balls
3	Quinoa Breakfast Cereal	Chicken Tetrazzini	Quinoa Tabbouleh	Spicy Pumpkin Seeds	Date-Pistachio Granola Bars
4	Milk with Peaches quinoa	Cauliflower Chicken Fried "Rice	Walnut-Rosemary Crusted Salmon	Spicy Pumpkin Seeds	Crispy Peanut Butter Balls
5	Overnight Light Peanut Butter Oats	Asparagus Tofu Stir-Fry	Turkey and Vegetable Barley Soup	Chia Seed Protein Bites	Peanut Butter-Oat Energy Balls
6	Multigrain Chia Waffles	Tuna Nicoise Salad	Red Pepper & Parmesan Tilapia	Cinnamon Popcorn	Flourless Banana Chocolate Chip Mini Muffins
7	Poached Eggs	Vegetarian Linguine	Asparagus Tofu Stir-Fry	Chia Seed Protein Bites	Date & Pistachio Bites

18.5 Week 5

Day	Breakfast	Lunch	Dinner	Snacks	Dessert
1	Milk with Peaches quinoa	Tomato Walnut Tilapia	Roast Chicken & Sweet Potato	Spicy Pumpkin Seeds	Apricot-Sunflower Granola Bars
2	Overnight Light Peanut Butter Oats	Broccoli Tuna Casserole	Red Pepper Chicken	Ocean Water	Flourless Banana Chocolate Chip Mini Muffins
3	Multigrain Chia Waffles	Walnut-Rosemary Crusted Salmon	Maple-Glazed Chicken Breasts	Chia Seed Protein Bites	Date & Pistachio Bites
4	Avocado-Egg Toast	Spanish Rice	Red Beans and Rice with Chicken	Cinnamon Popcorn	Peanut Butter-Oat Energy Balls
5	Quinoa Breakfast Cereal	Greek Sloppy Joes	Chicken-Noodle Casserole	Blueberry Smoothie	Date-Pistachio Granola Bars
6	Multigrain Chia Waffles	Beef & Bulgur-Stuffed Zucchini Boats	Chicken Tetrazzini	Avocado Smoothie with Leafy Greens	Crispy Peanut Butter Balls
7	Poached Eggs	California Burger Wraps	Red Beans and Rice with Chicken	Chocolate Shake	Carrot Cake Energy Bites

18.6 Week 6

Day	Breakfast	Lunch	Dinner	Snacks	Dessert
1	Overnight Light Peanut Butter Oats	Spanish Rice	Chickpea & Potato Curry	Avocado Smoothie with Leafy Greens	Crispy Peanut Butter Balls
2	Multigrain Chia Waffles	Zucchini Lasagna	Zucchini & Mushroom Sauté	Chocolate Shake	Carrot Cake Energy Bites
3	Avocado-Egg Toast	Spicy Chicken Pumpkin Pizza	Salmon with Horseradish Pistachio Crust	Spicy Pumpkin Seeds	Apricot-Sunflower Granola Bars
4	Quinoa Breakfast Cereal	Chicken and Broccoli with Dill Sauce	Cauliflower Pizza with Basil Pesto	Ocean Water	Flourless Banana Chocolate Chip Mini Muffins
5	Multigrain Chia Waffles	Tomato Walnut Tilapia	Cumin Quinoa Patties	Chia Seed Protein Bites	Date & Pistachio Bites
6	Poached Eggs	Juicy & Delicious Mixed Spice-Burgers	Spinach Quesadillas	Spicy Pumpkin Seeds	Peanut Butter-Oat Energy Balls
7	Milk with Peaches quinoa	Tropical Chicken Cauliflower Rice Bowls	Creamy Chicken Rice Soup	Spicy Pumpkin Seeds	Date-Pistachio Granola Bars

18.7 Week 7

Day	Breakfast	Lunch	Dinner	Snacks	Dessert
1	Milk with Overnight Oats	Chickpea & Potato Curry	Tomato Walnut Tilapia	Avocado Smoothie with Leafy Greens	Crispy Peanut Butter Balls
2	Apple Muffins	Zucchini & Mushroom Sauté	Broccoli Tuna Casserole	Chocolate Shake	Blueberry-Lemon Energy Balls
3	Lemon Avocado Toast	Salmon with Horseradish Pistachio Crust	Walnut-Rosemary Crusted Salmon	Spicy Pumpkin Seeds	Banana Energy Bites
4	Spinach Egg White Muffins	Cauliflower Pizza with Basil Pesto	Spanish Rice	Ocean Water	Peanut Butter-Oat Energy Balls
5	Overnight Light Peanut Butter Oats	Cumin Quinoa Patties	Greek Sloppy Joes	Chia Seed Protein Bites	Date & Pistachio Bites
6	Milk with Peaches quinoa	Spinach Quesadillas	Beef & Bulgur-Stuffed Zucchini Boats	Spicy Pumpkin Seeds	Carrot Cake Energy Bites
7	Breakfast Egg Salad	Creamy Chicken Rice Soup	California Burger Wraps	Spicy Pumpkin Seeds	Fruit Energy Balls

18.8 Week 8

Day	Breakfast	Lunch	Dinner	Snacks	Dessert
1	Pumpkin Spice Smoothie	Greek Sloppy Joes	Garlicky Shrimp & Broccoli	Spicy Pumpkin Seeds	Fruit Energy Balls
2	Poached Eggs	Beef & Bulgur-Stuffed Zucchini Boats	Red Pepper Chicken	Chia Seed Protein Bites	Apricot-Sunflower Granola Bars
3	Breakfast Cereal	Chicken Tetrazzini	California Burger Wraps	Cinnamon Popcorn	Date-Pistachio Granola Bars
4	Banana Nut Muffins	Cauliflower Chicken Fried "Rice	Lemony Parsley Baked Cod	Shrimp Cocktail	Carrot Cake Energy Bites
5	Overnight Light Peanut Butter Oats	Cumin Quinoa Patties	Greek Sloppy Joes	Chia Seed Protein Bites	Date & Pistachio Bites
6	Milk with Peaches quinoa	Spinach Quesadillas	Beef & Bulgur-Stuffed Zucchini Boats	Spicy Pumpkin Seeds	Carrot Cake Energy Bites
7	Breakfast Egg Salad	Creamy Chicken Rice Soup	California Burger Wraps	Spicy Pumpkin Seeds	Fruit Energy Balls

18.9 Week 9

Day	Breakfast	Lunch	Dinner	Snacks	Dessert
1	Overnight Light Peanut Butter Oats	Spanish Rice	Chickpea & Potato Curry	Avocado Smoothie with Leafy Greens	Crispy Peanut Butter Balls
2	Multigrain Chia Waffles	Zucchini Lasagna	Zucchini & Mushroom Sauté	Chocolate Shake	Carrot Cake Energy Bites
3	Avocado-Egg Toast	Spicy Chicken Pumpkin Pizza	Salmon with Horseradish Pistachio Crust	Spicy Pumpkin Seeds	Apricot-Sunflower Granola Bars
4	Quinoa Breakfast Cereal	Chicken and Broccoli with Dill Sauce	Cauliflower Pizza with Basil Pesto	Ocean Water	Flourless Banana Chocolate Chip Mini Muffins
5	Multigrain Chia Waffles	Tomato Walnut Tilapia	Cumin Quinoa Patties	Chia Seed Protein Bites	Date & Pistachio Bites
6	Poached Eggs	Juicy & Delicious Mixed Spice-Burgers	Spinach Quesadillas	Spicy Pumpkin Seeds	Peanut Butter-Oat Energy Balls
7	Milk with Peaches quinoa	Tropical Chicken Cauliflower Rice Bowls	Creamy Chicken Rice Soup	Spicy Pumpkin Seeds	Date-Pistachio Granola Bars

18.10 Week 10

Day	Breakfast	Lunch	Dinner	Snacks	Dessert
1	Lemon Avocado Toast	Chicken Salad	Stuffed Potatoes with Salsa & Beans	Chile-Lime Peanuts	Blueberry-Lemon Energy Balls
2	Milk with Peaches quinoa	Asparagus Tofu Stir-Fry	Lentil-Tomato Soup	Kale Chips	Banana Energy Bites
3	Overnight Light Peanut Butter Oats	Tuna Nicoise Salad	Shrimp and Cauliflower Bake	Horseradish Deviled Eggs	Date & Pistachio Bites
4	Multigrain Chia Waffles	Vegetarian Linguine	Creamy Chicken Rice Soup	Spicy Pumpkin Seeds	Fruit Energy Balls
5	Poached Eggs	Marinated Beet Salad	Walnut-Rosemary Crusted Salmon	Chia Seed Protein Bites	Apricot-Sunflower Granola Bars
6	Avocado-Egg Toast	Garlicky Green Beans	Turkey and Vegetable Barley Soup	Cinnamon Popcorn	Date-Pistachio Granola Bars
7	Quinoa Breakfast Cereal	Quinoa Tabbouleh	Red Pepper & Parmesan Tilapia	Shrimp Cocktail	Carrot Cake Energy Bites

19 Measurement Conversion Chart

Weight

Metric	Imperial
15 g	½ oz.
30 g	1 oz.
60g	2 oz.
90 g	3 oz.
125g	4oz.
175g	6 oz.
250g	8 oz.
300g	10 oz.
375 g	12 oz.
400 g	13 oz.
425 g	14 oz.
500 g	1 lb
750 g	1½ lb
1 kg	2lb

Liquid Measures

Quantity	Metric
1 teaspoon	5ml
1 tablespoon	15 ml
¼ cup	60 ml
1/3 cup	80 ml
½ cup	125 ml
1 cup	250 ml
1-¼ cup	300 ml
1½ cup	375 ml
1-2/3 cup	400 ml
1¾ cup	450 ml
2 cups	500 ml
2½ cups	600 ml
3 cups	750 ml

20 Conclusion

Even if you have a family history of diabetes, type 2, you can still reduce your risk by leading a healthy lifestyle. If you have prediabetes and make changes to your lifestyle, you may be able to delay or prevent the onset of diabetes.

A healthy way of life consists of:

consuming wholesome food. Select foods that are higher in fiber and lower in calories and fat. Incorporate more vegetables, fruits, and whole grains into your diet.

getting moving Aim for 150 or more minutes per week of cardiovascular exercise that ranges from moderate to vigorous, such as a brisk walk, a bike ride, a run, or swimming.

shedding pounds. Through weight loss and management, prediabetes can be prevented from progressing to type 2 diabetes. If you have prediabetes, losing 7–10% of your body weight can help you avoid developing diabetes.

avoiding prolonged inactivity. Your risk of type 2 diabetes may rise if you spend a lot of time sitting still. Every 30 minutes, make an effort to get up and walk around for at least a few minutes.

Metformin (Fortamet, Glumetza, and other brands), an oral diabetic medicine, may be administered for persons with prediabetes to lower their risk of developing type 2 diabetes. This is typically recommended to older persons who are obese and unable to alter their lifestyles to lower blood sugar levels.

Printed in Great Britain
by Amazon